بسم الله الرحمن الرحيم

Imām ibn Qayyim al-Jawziyyah [d. 751H]

CHARACTERISTICS of the HYPOCRITES

being a tranlation of his work
'Sifāt al-Munāfiqīn'

دار السنة

"There is a sickness in their hearts and Allāh has increased their sickness."

[*al-Baqarah* (2): 10]

Characteristics of the Hypocrites

by Imām ibn Qayyim al-Jawziyyah

with an appendix from the work of al-Shanqīṭī

Translated from the original Arabic by Abū Rumaysah

دار السنة

Dār as-Sunnah Publishers
BIRMINGHAM

Second Edition published in Great Britain, June 2013 / Sha'ban 1434H
by Dār as-Sunnah Publishers

DĀR AS-SUNNAH PUBLISHERS
P.O. Box 9818, Birmingham, B11 4WA, United Kingdom

W: www.darassunnah.com
E: info@darassunnah.com
E: daar-us-sunnah@mail.com

British Library Cataloguing in publication Data.
A catalogue record for this book is available from the British Library.

Title: Characteristics of the Hypocrites
by Imām ibn Qayyim al-Jawziyyah
Translation by Abū Rumaysah

ISBN 1-904336-14-0
Paper-back

Published and Typeset by: Dār as-Sunnah Publishers
First Edition 1424 AH/2004 CE
Second Edition 1434 AH/2013 CE

Content

APPENDIX ONE

The Parable of the Hypocrites

APPENDIX TWO

Transliteration Table

Consonants. Arabic

initial: unexpressed medial and final:

ء ʾ	د d	ض ḍ	ك k
ب b	ذ dh	ط ṭ	ل l
ت t	ر r	ظ ẓ	م m
ث th	ز z	ع ʿ	ن n
ج j	س s	غ gh	هـ h
ح ḥ	ش sh	ف f	و w
خ kh	ص ṣ	ق q	ي y

Vowels, diphthongs, etc.

Short:	ـَ a	ـِ i	ـُ u
long:	ـَا ā	ـُو ū	ـِي ī
diphthongs:		ـَوْ aw	
		ـَيْ ay	

IBN QAYYIM AL-JAWZIYYAH

May Allāh have mercy upon him

His Name:

HE IS THE IMĀM, THE ḤĀFIẒ, the exegete, the legal jurist, Shaykh al-Islām: Abū 'Abdullāh Shamsu-d-Dīn Muḥammad Ibn Abū Bakr - better known as Ibn Qayyim al-Jawziyyah.

His Birth and Education:

He was born into a noble and knowledgeable family on 7th Safar 691H in the village of Zar', near Damascus, Syria.

From an early age he set about acquiring knowledge of the Islāmic sciences from the scholars of his time. Describing his desire for knowledge, al-Ḥāfiẓ Ibn Rajab, *Dhayl Ṭabaqāt-l-Ḥanābilah* [4/449] said, 'He had an intense love for knowledge, for books, publications and writings.'

Ibn Kathīr, *al-Bidāyah wa-n-Nihāyah* [14/235] said, 'He acquired from such books what others could not acquire, and he developed a deep understanding of the books of the Salaf and of the Khalaf.'

His Teachers and Shaykhs:

They include Shihāb an-Nāblusī, Qāḍī Taqī ad-Dīn ibn Sulaymān, from whom he studied ḥadīth; Qāḍī Badr ad-Dīn ibn Jamā'ah; Ṣafī ad-Dīn al-Hindī; Ismā'īl ibn Muḥammad al-Ḥarrānī, from whom he studied fiqh and usūl; and also his father, from whom he learnt the laws of inheritance.

However, the most notable of his teachers was Shaykh al-Islām Ibn Taymiyyah, whom he accompanied and studied under for sixteen years. Al-Ḥāfiẓ Ibn Kathīr (14/234) said, 'He attained great proficiency in many branches of knowledge; particularly knowledge of tafsīr, ḥadīth, and usūl. When shaykh Taqī ad-Dīn ibn Taymiyyah returned from Egypt in the year 712H, he stayed with the shaykh until he died; learning a great deal of knowledge from him, along with the knowledge that he had already occupied himself in attaining. So he became a unique scholar in many branches of knowledge.'

His Manners and Worship:

Many of his students and contemporaries have born witness to his excellent character and his manners of worship. Ibn Rajab (4/450) said,

> He - may Allāh have mercy on him - was constant in worship and performing the night prayer, reaching the limits in lengthening his prayer and devotion. He was

> constantly in a state of *dhikr* and had an intense love for Allāh. He also had a deep love for turning to Allāh in repentance, humbling himself to Him with a deep sense of humility and helplessness. He would throw himself at the doors of Divine obedience and servitude. Indeed, I have not seen the likes of him with regards to such matters.

Ibn Kathīr (14/234) said,

> He was constant in humbly entreating and calling upon his Lord. He recited well and had fine manners. He had a great deal of love and did not harbour any envy or malice towards anyone, nor did he seek to harm or find fault with them. I was one of those who most often kept company with him and was one of the most beloved of people to him. I do not know of anyone in the world in this time, who is a greater worshipper than him. His prayer used to be very lengthy, with prolonged bowing and prostrations. His colleagues would criticise him for this, yet he never retorted back, nor did he abandon this practice. May Allāh bestow His mercy upon him.

His Students and Works:

Amongst his most prominent students were: Ibn Kathīr (d.774H), adh-Dhahabī (d.748H), Ibn Rajab (d.751H) and Ibn 'Abdu-l-Hādī (d.744H), as well as two of his sons, Ibrāhīm and Sharafu-d-Dīn 'Abdullāh.

Ibnu-l-Qayyim authored over sixty works. His books and writings are characterised by their touching address to the heart and soul, as well as their accuracy, precision, strength of argument and depth of research.

In the field of fiqh and usūl, his writings include: *Iʿlīmu-l-Muwaqqiḇīn; Turuqu-l-Ḥukmiyyah; Ighāthatu-l-Lahfān; Tuḥfatu-l-Mawlūd; Aḥkām Ahlu-l-Dhimmah*; and *al-Furūsiyyah*.

In the field of ḥadīth and sīrah they include: *Tahdhīb Sunan Abī Dāwūd; al-Manāru-l-Munīf; Fawā'id al-Ḥadīthiyyah; Jalā'u-l-Afhām; and Zādu-l-Maʿād.*

In the field of beliefs: *Ijtimāʿ al-Juyūsh al-lslāmiyyah; as-Ṣawāʿiqu-l-Mursalah; Shifāʿu-l-ʿAlīl; Ḥādiyu-l-Arwāḥ; al-Kāfiyatu-sh-Shāfiyah*; and *Kitāb ar-Rūḥ*.

In the field of akhlāq (morals) and tazkiyah (purification): *Madāriju-s-Sālikīn; ad-Dā' wa-d-Dawā'; al-Wābilu-s-Ṣayyib; al-Fawā'id; Risālatu-t-Tabūkiyyah; Miftāḥ Dār as-Saʿādah*; and *ʿUddatu-s-Ṣābirīn.*

In the sciences of the Qur'ān: *at-Tibyān fī Aqsāmi-l-Qur'ān*; and *Amthāl al-Qur'ān.*

In language and miscellaneous issues: *Badā'i al-Fawā'id.*

Two books have also been written collating the exegetical comments of ibn al-Qayyim from his various works: *Tafsīr al-Qayyim* and *Tafsīr al-Munīr.*

A few of his works have also been translated into the English language: the Magnificent Journey; the Invocation of God; Medicine of the Prophet; *Zād al-Maʿād.*

Statements of the Scholars about him:

Ibn Rajab (4/44) said,

> He had deep knowledge concerning tafsīr and the fundamentals of the religion, reaching the highest degree concerning them both. Similar was the case in the field of ḥadīth, with regards to understanding its meanings, subtleties and deducing rulings from them. Likewise was the case in the field of fiqh and its usūl, as well as the Arabic language. He did a great service to these sciences. He was also knowledgeable about rhetoric, grammar, and *sulūk* as well as the subtleties and details that occur in the speech of the people of *tasawwuf.*

Al-Ḥāfiẓ Ibn Ḥajar, *ad-Duraru-l-Kāminah* (4/21),

> He possessed a courageous spirit as well as vast and comprehensive knowledge. He had deep knowledge concerning the differences of opinions of the Scholars and about the ways of the Salaf.

Ibn Ḥajar also said in his commendation to ar-Raddu-l-Wāfir,

> And if there were no virtues of shaykh Taqī ad-Dīn [Ibn Taymiyyah], except for his famous student, shaykh Shamsu-d-Dīn ibn Qayyim al-Jawziyyah - the author of many works, which both his opponents and supporters benefited from - this would be a sufficient indication of his [Ibn Taymiyyah's] great position.

al-Ḥāfiẓ Ibn Nāṣir ad-Dimishqī, *ar-Raddu-l-Wāfir* [p. 69] said,

> He possessed knowledge of the sciences, especially tafsīr and usūl.

He also said:

> Abū Bakr Muḥammad Ibn al-Muhib said, as found in his letter, "I said in front of our Shaykh, al-Mizzī, 'Is Ibnu-l-Qayyim at the same level as Ibn Khuzaymah?' He replied, 'He is in this time, what Ibn Khuzaymah was in his time.'"

As-Suyūṭī, *Bughyatu-l-Wiʿāt* [1/62] said,

> His books had no equal and he strove and became one of the great Imāms in [the field of] tafsīr, ḥadīth, the Book, the Sunnah, furūʿ, and the Arabic language.

ʿAlī al-Qārī, *al-Mirqāt* [8/251],

> It will be clear to whoever aspires to read the explanation of *Manāzilu-s-Sā'irīn* [i.e. *Madārij as-Sālikīn*], that they [Ibn Taymiyyah and Ibnu-l-Qayyim] are from the great ones of *Ahlu-s-Sunnah wa-l-Jamāʿah*, and from the *awliyā'* of this Ummah.

Qāḍī Burhān ad-Dīn az-Zurʿā said as quoted from him in *Dhayl Ṭabaqāt al-Ḥanābilah,*

> There is none under the heavens who has greater knowledge than he.

His Death:

Imām Ibnu-l-Qayyim passed away at the age of sixty, on the 13th night of Rajab, 751H, may Allāh shower His Mercy upon him.

Characteristics of the Hypocrites

All praise and thanks are due to Allāh, we praise Him, ask His aid, and ask His forgiveness. We take refuge with Allāh from the evil of our souls and the evil of our deeds. Whoever Allāh guides, none can misguide; and whoever Allāh leaves to stray, none can guide. I bear witness that none has the right to be worshipped save Allāh and I bear witness that Muḥammad is His servant and Messenger.

يَٰٓأَيُّهَا ٱلَّذِينَ ءَامَنُوا۟ ٱتَّقُوا۟ ٱللَّهَ حَقَّ تُقَاتِهِۦ وَلَا تَمُوتُنَّ إِلَّا وَأَنتُم
مُّسْلِمُونَ ﴿١٠٢﴾

You who have faith! Fear Allāh as is truly due Him and do not die except as Muslims.

[*Āli 'Imrān* (3): 102]

يَٰٓأَيُّهَا ٱلنَّاسُ ٱتَّقُوا۟ رَبَّكُمُ ٱلَّذِى خَلَقَكُم مِّن نَّفْسٍ وَٰحِدَةٍ وَخَلَقَ مِنْهَا
زَوْجَهَا وَبَثَّ مِنْهُمَا رِجَالًا كَثِيرًا وَنِسَآءً ۚ وَٱتَّقُوا۟ ٱللَّهَ ٱلَّذِى تَسَآءَلُونَ
بِهِۦ وَٱلْأَرْحَامَ ۚ إِنَّ ٱللَّهَ كَانَ عَلَيْكُمْ رَقِيبًا ﴿١﴾

O mankind! Fear your Lord who created you from a single soul and created its mate from it and then disseminated many men and women from the two of them. Fear Allāh in whose name you make demands of one another and also in respect of your families. Allāh watches over you continually.

[*an-Nisā'* (4): 1]

يَٰٓأَيُّهَا ٱلَّذِينَ ءَامَنُوا۟ ٱتَّقُوا۟ ٱللَّهَ وَقُولُوا۟ قَوْلًا سَدِيدًا ﴿٧٠﴾ يُصْلِحْ
لَكُمْ أَعْمَٰلَكُمْ وَيَغْفِرْ لَكُمْ ذُنُوبَكُمْ ۗ وَمَن يُطِعِ ٱللَّهَ وَرَسُولَهُۥ
فَقَدْ فَازَ فَوْزًا عَظِيمًا ﴿٧١﴾

You who have faith! Fear Allāh and speak words that hit the mark. He will put your actions right for you and forgive you your wrong deeds. All who obey Allāh and His Messenger have won a mighty victory.

[*al-Aḥzāb* (33): 70-71]

Hypocrisy is a deep rooted and all-pervading spiritual disease. A person's heart could be overflowing with it yet be oblivious of it due to its hidden and subtle nature; frequently does it lead a person to think he is acting rightly when in reality he is spreading corruption. It is of two types: major and minor; major hypocrisy leads to eternal punishment in the lowest depths of Hell;[1] it is to outwardly display faith in Allāh, His Angels, His Books, His Messengers and the Last Day whereas inwardly one is devoid of such belief, indeed disbelieving in it. He does not believe that Allāh spoke to a man amongst men who He appointed to be a Messenger: guiding them by His permission and warning them of His punishment.

[1] Allāh, Exalted is He says, *"The hypocrites are in the lowest level of Hell and you will not find anyone to help them."* [*an-Nisā'* (4): 145]

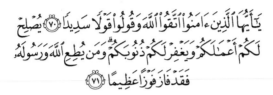

In the Qur'ān, Allāh has revealed the machinations of the hypocrites, He has unveiled their beliefs, their qualities, and made their goals clear so that the believers can be aware of them.[2] He divided mankind into three groups in the beginning of *Sūrah al-Baqarah*: the believer, the disbeliever, and the hypocrite. He mentioned four verses concerning the believers, two verses concerning the disbelievers, and thirteen verses concerning the hypocrites due to their plenitude and the great harm and tribulation they bring to Islām and the Muslims.[3] The harm they cause to Islām is truly severe for they claim to be Muslims, they claim to aid and support Islām, whereas in reality they are its enemies seeking to destroy it from within, covertly spreading their corruption and ignorance such that the unwary thinks that what they are upon is knowledge and right action.

By Allāh! How many strongholds of Islām have they destroyed; how many fortresses have they rendered to ruin; how many signposts of Islām have they effaced; how many raised flags have they lowered; and how many seeds of doubt have they attempted to sow in order to uproot the religion!

Islām and the Muslims have always faced trial and tribulation from them, wave after wave of doubts do they assault at it, all the while thinking that they are doing right,

أَلَآ إِنَّهُمْ هُمُ ٱلْمُفْسِدُونَ وَلَٰكِن لَّا يَشْعُرُونَ ﴿١٢﴾

[2] Allāh, Exalted is He says, *"The hypocrites are afraid that a chapter may be sent down about them, informing them of what is in their hearts. Say: 'Go on mocking! Allāh will expose everything you are afraid of!'"* [*at-Tawbah* (9): 64]

[3] As stated by Mujāhid amongst others. Refer to as-Suyūṭī, *ad-Durr al-Manthūr* [1/56].

> No indeed! They are the corrupters but they are not aware of it.
>
> [*al-Baqarah* (2): 12]

يُرِيدُونَ لِيُطْفِـُٔوا۟ نُورَ ٱللَّهِ بِأَفْوَٰهِهِمْ وَٱللَّهُ مُتِمُّ نُورِهِۦ وَلَوْ كَرِهَ ٱلْكَـٰفِرُونَ ﴿٨﴾

> They desire to extinguish Allāh's light with their mouths but Allāh will perfect His light though the disbelievers hate it.
>
> [*as-Ṣaff* (61): 8][4]

having agreed to abandon the revelation and follow a course other than the one directed by it,

فَتَقَطَّعُوٓا۟ أَمْرَهُم بَيْنَهُمْ زُبُرًا ۖ كُلُّ حِزْبٍۭ بِمَا لَدَيْهِمْ فَرِحُونَ ﴿٥٣﴾

> But they disagreed and split up, dividing into sects, each party exulting in what it had.
>
> [*al-Mu'minūn* (23): 53]

يُوحِى بَعْضُهُمْ إِلَىٰ بَعْضٍ زُخْرُفَ ٱلْقَوْلِ غُرُورًا ۚ

> ...who inspire each other with delusions by means of specious words.
>
> [*al-An'ām* (6): 112]

---

[4] as-Sa'dī, *Taysīr al-Karīm ar-Raḥmān* said, "It is Allāh who has undertaken the task of aiding His religion, perfecting the truth with which He sent His Messengers, and manifesting its light in all regions of the earth, even though the disbelievers hate it. Even though they strive to the utmost of their abilities to extinguish His light, defeat and failure is their fate. They are like a person who blows air with his mouth in the direction of the sun in the hope that he can extinguish its fire: never will he be able to do so, rather he just imputes his own intellect with deficiency and doltishness."

and because of this,

اتَّخَذُوا هَٰذَا الْقُرْءَانَ مَهْجُورًا ﴿٣٠﴾

...they took this Qur'ān as something to be ignored.
[*al-Furqān* (25):30]

The characteristics of faith are not to be found in their hearts and hence they do not know them; oblivious are they to its pillars and hence do not take care of them; extinguished are the brilliant lights of its stars in their hearts and they do not try to relight them, and the darkness of their thoughts and beliefs has eclipsed the sun of faith such that they no longer see it. They do not accept the guidance of Allāh with which He sent His Messengers, they attach no importance to it, and they see nothing wrong in leaving it for their own opinions and beliefs. They have wrenched the texts of revelation of their true status, they have detached them of their importance and definitiveness, and they have submerged them in the obscurity of false interpretations. Subterfuge after subterfuge do they launch against these texts, and it is as if they face them in the same way an unwilling host meets malevolent guests: devoid of acceptance and generosity, all the while forcing himself to host them, yet keeping his distance. They say to these texts, 'You have no way to pass by us,' and if they find no option but to accept them, they do so by propounding multifarious plots and concocting various principles. When these texts find way past their doors, they say, 'What have we to do with their literal meanings, they give us no certainty whatsoever!' and the general masses amongst them say, 'Sufficient for us is what we find the latter people upon for they were more knowledgeable than the Righteous Predecessors, and firmer and more rightly guided in knowing the proofs and evidences!' In their view the way of the Salaf is the way of simplicity and soundness of heart because they did not busy themselves with investigating and laying out the principles of rhetoric; instead they merely devoted themselves to doing the obligatory and leaving the prohibited. Therefore the way of the latter people is more deeply rooted in knowledge and wiser whereas the way of the Salaf is greater in ignorance but safer.[5]

They treat the texts of the Book and Sunnah like the Khalīfah is treated in these times: while his name is written on coins and gains superficial mention in the Friday sermons, he has no real authority and it is other men who govern, his judgment is neither heard nor adhered to. They have donned the robes of the people of faith which cover their hearts of misguidance, deception and disbelief. Their tongues are the tongues of Muslims but their hearts are the hearts of those fighting them. They say,

ءَامَنَّا بِٱللَّهِ وَبِٱلْيَوْمِ ٱلْـَٔاخِرِ وَمَا هُم بِمُؤْمِنِينَ ﴿٨﴾

> 'We have faith in Allāh and the Last Day' - but they are not believers.
>
> [*al-Baqarah* (2): 8][6]

Their capital is deception and scheming, their merchandise is

---

[5] Allāh, Exalted is He says, *"Look how they invent lies against Allāh. That suffices as an outright felony!"* [*an-Nisā'* (4): 50]

[6] This verse then describes the first characteristic of hypocrisy: lying. They say with their tongues that which is not in their hearts. This quality is so entrenched in them that even when they spoke words that were true, Allāh still called them liars because what they said did not conform to what they believed, *"When the hypocrites come to you they say, 'We bear witness that you are indeed the Messenger of Allāh.' Allāh knows that you are indeed His Messenger and Allāh bears witness that the hypocrites are certainly liars."* [*al-Munāfiqūn* (63): 1]. Refer to the commentary of ibn Kathīr to this verse.

lies and treachery, and their intellect is one that is employed just for this world: believers and disbelievers alike are happy with them and they live in security amongst both,

يُخَٰدِعُونَ ٱللَّهَ وَٱلَّذِينَ ءَامَنُوا۟ وَمَا يَخْدَعُونَ إِلَّآ أَنفُسَهُمْ وَمَا يَشْعُرُونَ ﴿٩﴾

They think to deceive Allāh and those who believe but they deceive none save themselves but they are not aware of it.

[*al-Baqarah* (2): 9][7]

The disease of desires and doubts has consumed their hearts and destroyed them, and evil objectives have permeated their motivations and intentions and corrupted them. Their corrup-

[7] This verse describes the second characteristic of the hypocrites: their ignorance of Allāh for they try to deceive One who cannot be deceived, One who knows what they manifest and what they hide! This verse also shows their deceptive qualities, their third characteristic, as well as their making mockery of the religion and looking down on it. As-Sa'dī said, "Deception is to show the one being deceived something and hide the reality in order to reach ones goal. The hypocrites tried to deal with Allāh and the believers in this way but their deception came back on themselves. This is something extraordinary for normally a deceiver will either be successful and see the fruition of his goal, or at least be safe. These hypocrites did what they did, and plotted their plans, but all they succeeded in doing was seal their own destruction."

At-Ṭabarī mentions that Allāh deceives them in this world, *"The disbelievers should not imagine that the extra time We grant them is good for them. We only allow them more time so they will increase in evildoing. They will have a humiliating punishment."* [*Āli 'Imrān* (3): 178] and in the Hereafter, *"That Day when the men and women of the hypocrites will say to those who have faith, 'Wait for us so that we can borrow some of your light.' They will be told, 'Go back and look for light!' And a wall well be erected between them with a gate in it, on the inside of which there will be mercy and before whose exterior lies punishment."* [*al-Ḥadīd* (57): 13]

tion is so severe that they are flung to perdition, and the doctors of the religion are unable to cure them,

فِي قُلُوبِهِم مَّرَضٌ فَزَادَهُمُ ٱللَّهُ مَرَضًا
وَلَهُمْ عَذَابٌ أَلِيمٌۢ بِمَا كَانُوا۟ يَكْذِبُونَ ﴿١٠﴾

> There is a sickness in their hearts and Allāh has increased their sickness. They will have a painful punishment on account of their lies.
>
> [*al-Baqarah* (2): 10][8]

Whoever falls prey to the claws of their doubts will have his faith shredded to pieces; whoever allows his heart to open to their vile tribulations will find himself in a burning furnace; and whoever lends an ear to their deceptions will find them coming between him and firm belief. Indeed the corruption they cause on earth is great but most people are unaware,

---

[8] This verse describes their fourth characteristic: they are plagued with the disease of doubts and desires. As-Sa'dī said, "The sickness here is the sickness of doubts and desires. The heart is beset by two diseases that eject it from its state of balance and normalcy: the disease of false doubts and the disease of vile desires. Disbelief, hypocrisy, doubts, and innovations all arise from the disease of doubts. Fornication, the love of lewd deeds, and sins all arise from the disease of desire... This verse also shows that it is as a consequence of ones sins that Allāh punishes him by afflicting him with more sins."

At-Ṭabarī gives an example of how this verse was actualised by stating that each time a sūrah was revealed of the Qur'ān containing new injunctions, this increased them in their doubts and hence their disease increased, *"Each time a sūrah is revealed there are some among them who say, 'Which of you has this increased in faith?' As for those who believe, it increases their faith and they rejoice at it. But as for those with sickness in their hearts, it adds defilement to their defilement and they die as disbelievers."* [*at-Tawbah* (9): 124-125]

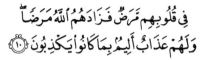

وَإِذَا قِيلَ لَهُمْ
لَا تُفْسِدُوا۟ فِى ٱلْأَرْضِ قَالُوٓا۟ إِنَّمَا نَحْنُ مُصْلِحُونَ ﴿١١﴾
أَلَآ إِنَّهُمْ هُمُ ٱلْمُفْسِدُونَ وَلَٰكِن لَّا يَشْعُرُونَ ﴿١٢﴾

When they are told, 'Do not cause corruption on the earth,' they say, 'We are only putting things right.' No indeed! They are the corrupters but they are not aware of it.

[*al-Baqarah* (2): 11-12][9]

When one of them follows the Book and Sunnah, he is doing so to keep up appearances, he is like a donkey carrying books: it understands none of what it is carrying. The revelation in their eyes is profitless merchandise and as such worthless. Those who truly follow it are fools in their eyes,

[9] This verse describes their fifth characteristic: spreading corruption in the land, a direct consequence of the corruption of their hearts. As-Sa'dī said, "When these hypocrites are prohibited from spreading corruption on the earth: acting by and promoting disbelief and sins, disclosing the plans and secrets of the Muslims to their enemies, and befriending the disbelievers; *"they say, 'We are only putting things right.'"* They combine spreading corruption on earth with making out that they are only putting things right, thereby altering reality and believing the falsehood they are on to be the truth. The crime of these is greater than the crime of one who just commits sins while believing them to be prohibited, for there is more hope that the latter person will retract and return. Now because their saying, *'We are only putting things right,'* serves to constrain right deeds to them, implying thereby that the deeds of the believers are not right or corrective; Allāh rebuts them by saying, *'No indeed! They are the corrupters,'* for there is no greater corruption than disbelieving in the verses and signs of Allāh, preventing people from His Way, trying to deceive Allāh and His friends, and befriending the enemies of Allāh and His Messenger."

وَإِذَا قِيلَ
لَهُمْ ءَامِنُوا۟ كَمَآ ءَامَنَ ٱلنَّاسُ قَالُوٓا۟ أَنُؤْمِنُ كَمَآ ءَامَنَ ٱلسُّفَهَآءُ ۗ
أَلَآ إِنَّهُمْ هُمُ ٱلسُّفَهَآءُ وَلَـٰكِن لَّا يَعْلَمُونَ ﴿١٣﴾

When they are told, 'Believe like the people have believed,' they say, 'What! Are we to believe like the fools have believed?' No indeed! They are the fools, but they do not know it.

[*al-Baqarah* (2): 13][10]

Each one of them has two faces: a face with which he meets the Muslims and a face with which he meets his deviated associates. Each one of them has two tongues: a false tongue with which he meets the Muslims and a true tongue which expresses his actual beliefs,

وَإِذَا لَقُوا۟
ٱلَّذِينَ ءَامَنُوا۟ قَالُوٓا۟ ءَامَنَّا وَإِذَا خَلَوْا۟ إِلَىٰ شَيَـٰطِينِهِمْ قَالُوٓا۟ إِنَّا
مَعَكُمْ إِنَّمَا نَحْنُ مُسْتَهْزِءُونَ ﴿١٤﴾

When they meet those who have believed they say, 'We have believed.' But when they go apart with their dev-

---

[10] This verse describes their sixth characteristic: their belittling the religion and those who follow it, and their foolishness. As-Sa'dī said, "Allāh informs us that they are the true fools because foolishness is defined by a person not knowing what is good for himself and his pursuing that which would harm him. These qualities are applicable to them. They way of intelligence and insight is for a person to know what is good for him and to pursue it and to repress what would harm him. These qualities are applicable to the Companions and the believers. Consideration is given to reality and not to mere claims and empty words."

> ils they say, 'We are really with you. We were only mocking.'
>
> [*al-Baqarah* (2): 14][11]

They have turned away from the Book and Sunnah, making mockery of those who follow them and looking down on them. They refuse to submit to the revelation, making do with what knowledge they have: and what knowledge? The increase of which only leads to more evil and arrogance! You will always see them mocking those who follow the clear import of the revelation but,[12]

ٱللَّهُ يَسْتَهْزِئُ بِهِمْ وَيَمُدُّهُمْ فِى طُغْيَٰنِهِمْ يَعْمَهُونَ ﴿١٥﴾

> Allāh is mocking them, and drawing them on, as they wander blindly in their excessive insolence.
>
> [*al-Baqarah* (2): 15]

They ply their trade in oceans of darkness traversing vessels of doubts. Uncertainty and suspicion plagues them as they sail through waves of illusion. Strong winds play havoc with their boats and lead them to their destruction,

[11] This is an example of their heinous lies, saying with their tongues what is not in their hearts, in order to acquire temporal gain.

Allāh, Exalted is He says, *"They try to conceal themselves from people, but they cannot conceal themselves from Allāh. He is with them when they spend the night saying things which are not pleasing to Him. Allāh encompasses everything they do."* [*an-Nisā'* (4): 108]

[12] Allāh, Exalted is He says, *"It has already been sent down to you in the Book that when you hear Allāh's Signs being rejected and mocked at by people, you must not sit with them till they start talking of other things. If you do not you are just the same as them. Allāh will gather the hypocrites and disbelievers in Hell altogether."* [*an-Nisā'* (4): 140]

أُوْلَٰٓئِكَ ٱلَّذِينَ ٱشْتَرَوُاْ ٱلضَّلَٰلَةَ
بِٱلْهُدَىٰ فَمَا رَبِحَت تِّجَٰرَتُهُمْ وَمَا كَانُواْ مُهْتَدِينَ ﴿١٦﴾

Those are people who have sold guidance for misguidance. Their trade has brought no profit and they are not guided.

[*al-Baqarah* (2): 16][13]

The fire of faith alights for them and in its light they perceive guidance and misguidance, then that fire is extinguished and is left as red hot ashes. With that fire are they punished and in that darkness do they wander blindly,

مَثَلُهُمْ كَمَثَلِ ٱلَّذِى ٱسْتَوْقَدَ نَارًا فَلَمَّآ أَضَآءَتْ مَا حَوْلَهُۥ
ذَهَبَ ٱللَّهُ بِنُورِهِمْ وَتَرَكَهُمْ فِى ظُلُمَٰتٍ لَّا يُبْصِرُونَ ﴿١٧﴾

Their example is that of people who light a fire, and then when it has lit up all round them, Allāh removes their light and leaves them in darkness, unable to see.

[*al-Baqarah* (2): 17]

---

[13] as-Sa'dī said, 'Meaning they desired that misguidance in the same way that a buyer desires a particular commodity so much so that he would give something precious as payment. This is an excellent similitude: misguidance, the worst evil, has been compared to the commodity; and guidance, the best of things, has been compared to the asking price. So they paid the price and gained what they desired, misguidance...what a wretched trade and what a disgraceful bargain! If someone gives a dīnār to get back a dirham, he feels that he has lost out, so what of one who gives a diamond and gets in return a dirham?! And what of one who chooses misery and anguish in place of felicity and bliss?!'

Allāh, Exalted is He gives an example of such a trade by saying, *"When the hypocrites and those with sickness in their hearts said, 'These people have been deluded by their religion.' But those who put their trust in Allāh will find Allāh to be Almighty, All-Wise."* [*al-Anfāl* (8): 50]

The hearing of their hearts is burdened by a heavy load and as such they are unable to hear the call to faith; the eyes of their spiritual sight are covered with a blinding wrapping such that they cannot see the realities of the Qur'ān; and their tongues are mute to the truth such that they are unable to speak it,

صُمٌّۢ بُكۡمٌ عُمۡيٌ فَهُمۡ لَا يَرۡجِعُونَ ﴿١٨﴾

Deaf, dumb, blind. They will not return.

[*al-Baqarah* (2): 18]

The rain of revelation pours down upon them, it contains life for the hearts and souls, but all they can hear of it is the thunder strikes of its threats, promises, and ordinances. They thrust their fingers in their ears and draw their garments over them, trying to run in earnest and desperately seeking their footprints so as to retreat. However they are summoned in public, and their secrets are made plain for all who can see, and two parables are propounded for them, each parable unveiling one of the two parties amongst them: those who debate and those who blindly follow.

أَوۡ كَصَيِّبٖ مِّنَ ٱلسَّمَآءِ فِيهِ
ظُلُمَٰتٞ وَرَعۡدٞ وَبَرۡقٞ يَجۡعَلُونَ أَصَٰبِعَهُمۡ فِيٓ ءَاذَانِهِم مِّنَ ٱلصَّوَٰعِقِ
حَذَرَ ٱلۡمَوۡتِۚ وَٱللَّهُ مُحِيطُۢ بِٱلۡكَٰفِرِينَ ﴿١٩﴾

Or that of a storm-cloud in the sky, full of darkness, thunder and lightning. They put their fingers in their ears against the thunderclaps, fearful of death. Allāh encompasses the disbelievers.

[*al-Baqarah* (2): 19]

Their spiritual sight is too weak to bear what the rain contains:

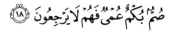

the lightning of its radiant proofs and the brightness of its meanings. Their ears are unable to accept the thunder strikes of its promises, orders, and prohibitions; as such they come to a halt in confusion, their faculty of hearing brings them no benefit and their sight is unable to guide them,

يَكَادُ ٱلْبَرْقُ يَخْطَفُ
أَبْصَٰرَهُمْ كُلَّمَآ أَضَآءَ لَهُم مَّشَوْاْ فِيهِ وَإِذَآ أَظْلَمَ عَلَيْهِمْ قَامُواْ
وَلَوْ شَآءَ ٱللَّهُ لَذَهَبَ بِسَمْعِهِمْ وَأَبْصَٰرِهِمْ إِنَّ ٱللَّهَ عَلَىٰ كُلِّ
شَىْءٍ قَدِيرٌ ﴿٢٠﴾

The lightning all but takes away their sight. Whenever they have light, they walk therein but whenever darkness covers them, they halt. If Allāh wished, He could take away their hearing and sight. Allāh has power over all things.

[al-Baqarah (2): 20][14]

They have characteristic signs by which they can be known, explained in the Book and the Sunnah, and clear for all those who are enriched with faith to see. They are people, by Allāh, given to ostentation, and this is the worst station that man can reach. They are a people prone to laziness and laxity in fulfilling the orders of the All-Merciful, and because of this they find sincerity burdensome,

---

[14] The author, may Allāh have mercy upon him, has a detailed explanation to both these parables in his *Ijtimāʾ al-Juyūsh al-Islāmiyyah*, this can be read in Appendix 1; Appendix 2 contains a beneficial explanation to the second parable by Muḥammad Amīn ash-Shanqīṭī.

وَإِذَا قَامُوٓاْ إِلَى
ٱلصَّلَوٰةِ قَامُواْ كُسَالَىٰ يُرَآءُونَ ٱلنَّاسَ وَلَا يَذْكُرُونَ ٱللَّهَ إِلَّا
قَلِيلًا ﴿١٤٢﴾

> When they get up to pray, they get up lazily, showing off to people, and only remembering Allāh a little.
> [*an-Nisā'* (4):142][15]

They are like a sheep that has strayed and finds itself between two flocks, it goes to one and then the other and does not stay with any of them. They are standing between two groups of people, all the while searching as to which is the stronger and nobler,

مُّذَبْذَبِينَ بَيْنَ ذَٰلِكَ لَآ إِلَىٰ هَٰٓؤُلَآءِ وَلَآ إِلَىٰ هَٰٓؤُلَآءِ
وَمَن يُضْلِلِ ٱللَّهُ فَلَن تَجِدَ لَهُۥ سَبِيلًا ﴿١٤٣﴾

> They vacillate between the two, not joining these or joining those. If Allāh misguides someone, you will not find any way for him to go.
> [*an-Nisā'* (4): 143]

They are on the lookout to see what happens to Ahlus-Sunnah; if victory comes their way they say, 'Were we not with you?' and they swear their strongest oaths by Allāh on this. If victory goes to the enemies of *Ahlus-Sunnah* they say to them 'Do you not know that we have a binding pact of brotherhood with you,' ' and

[15] Allāh also says about them, *"Nothing prevents what they give from being accepted from them but the fact that they have rejected Allāh and His Messenger, and that they come to prayer lethargically, and that they only give reluctantly."* [*at-Tawbah* (9): 54]

they bring their closeness of lineage as proof for this.[16] Whoever wishes to know them, let him take their descriptions from the words of the Lord of the worlds, and after that he will require no further proof,

ٱلَّذِينَ يَتَرَبَّصُونَ بِكُمْ فَإِن كَانَ لَكُمْ فَتْحٌ مِّنَ ٱللَّهِ قَالُوٓا۟ أَلَمْ
نَكُن مَّعَكُمْ وَإِن كَانَ لِلْكَٰفِرِينَ نَصِيبٌ قَالُوٓا۟ أَلَمْ نَسْتَحْوِذْ
عَلَيْكُمْ وَنَمْنَعْكُم مِّنَ ٱلْمُؤْمِنِينَ ۚ فَٱللَّهُ يَحْكُمُ بَيْنَكُمْ يَوْمَ
ٱلْقِيَٰمَةِ ۗ وَلَن يَجْعَلَ ٱللَّهُ لِلْكَٰفِرِينَ عَلَى ٱلْمُؤْمِنِينَ سَبِيلًا ﴿١٤١﴾

> Those who anticipate the worst for you say, 'Were we not with you?' whenever you gain a victory from Allāh, but if the disbelievers have a success they say, 'Did we not have the upper hand over you and yet in spite of that keep the believers away from you?' Allāh will judge between you on the Day of Judgment. Allāh will not give the disbelievers any way against the believers.
>
> [*an-Nisā'* (4): 141]

One who listens to them will be astounded by the silkiness and softness of their speech, he will bring Allāh to witness for what is in his heart of lies and deceit,

---

[16] Allāh, Exalted is He says, *"Give news to the hypocrites that they will have a painful punishment. Those who take the disbelievers as protectors rather than the believers, do they hope to find power and strength with them? Power and strength belong entirely to Allāh."* [*an-Nisā'* (4): 138-139]; *"You who have faith! Do not take the Jews and Christians as your friends; they are friends of one another. Any of you who takes them as friends is one of them and Allāh does not guide wrongdoing people. Yet you see those with sickness in their hearts rushing to them, saying, 'We fear the wheel of fate may turn against us.' But it may well be that Allāh will bring about victory or some other contingency from Him. Then they will deeply regret their secret thoughts."* [*al-Mā'idah* (5): 51-52]

وَمِنَ ٱلنَّاسِ مَن يُعۡجِبُكَ قَوۡلُهُۥ فِي ٱلۡحَيَوٰةِ ٱلدُّنۡيَا وَيُشۡهِدُ ٱللَّهَ عَلَىٰ مَا فِي قَلۡبِهِۦ وَهُوَ أَلَدُّ ٱلۡخِصَامِ ﴿٢٠٤﴾

> Among the people there is someone whose words about the worldly life excite your admiration, and he calls Allāh to witness what is in his heart, while he is in fact the most hostile of adversaries.
>
> [*al-Baqarah* (2): 204]

What they enjoin upon their followers entails corrupting them and spreading corruption in the land. What they prohibit their followers from entails what would be better for them in this life and the Hereafter. You would see one of them amongst the believers praying and remembering Allāh but,

وَإِذَا تَوَلَّىٰ سَعَىٰ فِي ٱلۡأَرۡضِ لِيُفۡسِدَ فِيهَا وَيُهۡلِكَ ٱلۡحَرۡثَ وَٱلنَّسۡلَۚ وَٱللَّهُ لَا يُحِبُّ ٱلۡفَسَادَ ﴿٢٠٥﴾

> When he leaves you, he goes about the earth corrupting it, destroying crops and animals. Allāh does not love corruption.
>
> [*al-Baqarah* (2): 205]

They are all similar, enjoining the evil after having committed it themselves and prohibiting the good after having left it themselves. They are miserly in giving their wealth in the way of Allāh, in ways that He loves it to be spent.[17] How many times has Allāh

---

[17] Allāh, Exalted is He says, "*Allāh does not love those who are vain or boastful. Those*
=

reminded them of the blessings He has conferred upon them yet they turn away and abandon Him! Listen, believers, to what He says about them,

ٱلْمُنَٰفِقُونَ وَٱلْمُنَٰفِقَٰتُ
بَعْضُهُم مِّنۢ بَعْضٍ ۚ يَأْمُرُونَ بِٱلْمُنكَرِ وَيَنْهَوْنَ
عَنِ ٱلْمَعْرُوفِ وَيَقْبِضُونَ أَيْدِيَهُمْ ۚ نَسُوا۟ ٱللَّهَ فَنَسِيَهُمْ ۗ
إِنَّ ٱلْمُنَٰفِقِينَ هُمُ ٱلْفَٰسِقُونَ ﴿٦٧﴾

> The men and women of the hypocrites are as bad as one another. They command what is wrong and forbid what is right and keep their fists tightly closed. They have forgotten Allāh so He has forgotten them. The hypocrites are deviators.
>
> [*at-Tawbah* (9): 67]

If you invite them to judge by the clear import of the revelation you will see them turn away in aversion. If you could see their reality you would see a vast gulf between them and the truth, and you would see the stringency with which they turn away from the revelation.

وَإِذَا قِيلَ لَهُمْ تَعَالَوْا۟ إِلَىٰ مَآ أَنزَلَ
ٱللَّهُ وَإِلَى ٱلرَّسُولِ رَأَيْتَ ٱلْمُنَٰفِقِينَ يَصُدُّونَ عَنكَ
صُدُودًا ﴿٦١﴾

=

who are tight-fisted and direct others to be tight-fisted and hide the bounty Allāh has given them. We have prepared a humiliating punishment for the disbelievers, and also for those who spend their wealth to show off to people, not having faith in Allāh and the Last Day." [*an-Nisā'* (4): 36-37]

When they are told, 'Come to what Allāh has sent down and to the Messenger,' you see the hypocrites turn away from you completely.

[*an-Nisā'* (4): 61][18]

How can they be successful and guided after their intellects and religion have been afflicted so, truly unlikely is it that they will be saved from the mire and misguidance they are in. They have bought disbelief at the expense of faith and what trade is there as profitless as this?! They have exchanged the choicest sealed wine for blazing fire,

فَكَيْفَ إِذَآ أَصَٰبَتْهُم مُّصِيبَةٌۢ بِمَا
قَدَّمَتْ أَيْدِيهِمْ ثُمَّ جَآءُوكَ يَحْلِفُونَ بِٱللَّهِ إِنْ أَرَدْنَآ إِلَّآ
إِحْسَٰنًا وَتَوْفِيقًا ﴿٦٢﴾

How will it be when a disaster strikes them because of what they have done, and then they come to you swearing by Allāh: 'We desired nothing but good and reconciliation.'

[*an-Nisā'* (4): 62]

The vileness of doubts and suspicion cling firmly to their hearts and they can find no way of absolution from them,

[18] The previous verse reads, *"Do you not see those who claim they have faith in what has been sent down to you and what has been sent down before you, still desiring to turn to a satanic source for judgment in spite of being ordered to reject it? Satan wants to misguide them far away."* [*an-Nisā'* (4): 60]

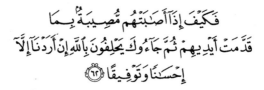

أُوْلَٰٓئِكَ ٱلَّذِينَ يَعْلَمُ ٱللَّهُ مَا
فِى قُلُوبِهِمْ فَأَعْرِضْ عَنْهُمْ وَعِظْهُمْ وَقُل لَّهُمْ فِىٓ
أَنفُسِهِمْ قَوْلًۢا بَلِيغًا ﴿٦٣﴾

...Allāh knows what is in such people's hearts so turn away from them and warn them and speak to them with words that take effect.

[*an-Nisāʾ* (4): 63]

May they perish! How distant they are from the reality of faith and how false their claim to cognisance is! They are one thing and the followers of the Messenger (ﷺ) are something totally different.

Allāh, Mighty and Magnificent, has taken an oath in His Book upon Himself; the greatness of which will be realised by those endowed with spiritual insight, those whose hearts are fearful of Him by way of magnification and exaltation. Allāh, Exalted is He, says, warning His friends and alerting us to the state of these people,

فَلَا وَرَبِّكَ لَا يُؤْمِنُونَ
حَتَّىٰ يُحَكِّمُوكَ فِيمَا شَجَرَ بَيْنَهُمْ ثُمَّ لَا يَجِدُواْ
فِىٓ أَنفُسِهِمْ حَرَجًا مِّمَّا قَضَيْتَ وَيُسَلِّمُواْ تَسْلِيمًا ﴿٦٥﴾

No, by your Lord, they are not believers until they make you their judge in the disputes that break out between them, and then find no resistance within themselves to what you decide and submit themselves completely.

[*an-Nisāʾ* (4): 65]

You will find one of them taking oaths before commencing his words, without anyone even objecting to what he says, because he knows that the hearts of the believers do not find tranquillity in what he says.[19] Therefore he uses the oath as a way of securing himself from any suspicions that may come his way. It is in the same way that people given to doubts and misgivings lie, making oaths in order to beguile the listener into thinking they are telling the truth,

ٱتَّخَذُوٓاْ أَيۡمَٰنَهُمۡ جُنَّةٗ فَصَدُّواْ عَن سَبِيلِ ٱللَّهِۚ إِنَّهُمۡ سَآءَ مَا كَانُواْ يَعۡمَلُونَ ﴿٢﴾

They made their oaths a cloak and barred the Way of Allāh. What they have done is truly evil.

[*al-Munāfiqūn* (63): 2]

May they perish! They embarked upon the journey across the great white plain with the caravan of faith, then seeing the length of the journey and how far its destination was made them turn on their heels and return. They think they have found a good life and they sleep comfortably in their beds, but neither in that life have they really lived, and neither in that slumber have they found any real benefit. It is not long till when a caller will give a single cry and they will all stand forth, leaving their life behind, hungry, not feeling any form of satiation... what will their state be at the time of the Meeting? They knew then they rejected, they saw the truth then they became blinded to it,

[19] Allāh, Exalted is He says, *"They swear to you by Allāh in order to please you, but it would have been more fitting for them to please and Allāh and His Messenger if they are believers. Do they not know that whoever opposes Allāh and His Messenger will have the Fire of Hell, remaining in it timelessly, for ever? That is the great disgrace."* [*at-Tawbah* (9): 62-63]

ذَٰلِكَ بِأَنَّهُمْ ءَامَنُوا۟ ثُمَّ كَفَرُوا۟ فَطُبِعَ عَلَىٰ قُلُوبِهِمْ
فَهُمْ لَا يَفْقَهُونَ ۝٣

That is because they have believed and returned to disbelief. So their hearts are sealed up and they cannot understand.

[*al-Munāfiqūn* (63): 3]

The best of men in physical appearance, the most enchanting of tongues, the nicest words, yet the most vile of hearts. They are like propped up planks of wood devoid of fruit. They have been severed from the source of their growth and as such rest on a wall to keep them upright so that people do not walk over them.

وَإِذَا رَأَيْتَهُمْ تُعْجِبُكَ أَجْسَامُهُمْ
وَإِن يَقُولُوا۟ تَسْمَعْ لِقَوْلِهِمْ كَأَنَّهُمْ خُشُبٌ مُّسَنَّدَةٌ يَحْسَبُونَ كُلَّ
صَيْحَةٍ عَلَيْهِمْ هُمُ ٱلْعَدُوُّ فَٱحْذَرْهُمْ قَـٰتَلَهُمُ ٱللَّهُ أَنَّىٰ يُؤْفَكُونَ ۝٤

When you see them, their outward form appeals to you, and if they speak you listen to what they say. But they are like propped-up planks of wood. They imagine every cry to be against them. They are the enemy, so beware of them. Allāh fight them! How they are perverted!

[*al-Munāfiqūn* (63): 4]

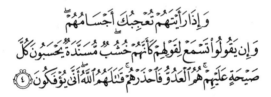

They delay the prayer to the last possible time: Fajr at sunrise and 'Aṣr at sunset at which time they quickly peck the ground as does a crow. This is because their prayer is a prayer in body but not of heart.[20] While praying they look left and right as does a fox being certain that it is being hunted and chased. They do not attend the congregational prayer, rather they make do with praying in their homes or shops. When they argue they behave uncouthly, when they are entrusted with something they break the trust, when they speak they lie, and when they promise they break it. This is how they deal with creation and Creator. Read their descriptions in the beginning of *al-Muṭaffifin* and the end of *at-Ṭariq* for none can describe to you the characteristics of someone better than one who knows him well,

يَـٰٓأَيُّهَا ٱلنَّبِىُّ جَـٰهِدِ ٱلْكُفَّارَ وَٱلْمُنَـٰفِقِينَ وَٱغْلُظْ عَلَيْهِمْ ۚ
وَمَأْوَىٰهُمْ جَهَنَّمُ ۖ وَبِئْسَ ٱلْمَصِيرُ ﴿٩﴾

> O Prophet! Do Jihād against the disbelievers and hypocrites and be harsh with them. Their refuge is Hell, what an evil destination.
>
> [*at-Taḥrīm* (66): 9]

They may think they are many but in reality they are few. They may think they are strong but in reality they are weak and despicable. They are ignoramuses thinking themselves high and mighty. They are misled about Allāh for they are ignorant of His greatness,

وَيَحْلِفُونَ بِٱللَّهِ إِنَّهُمْ لَمِنكُمْ وَمَا هُم مِّنكُمْ وَلَـٰكِنَّهُمْ
قَوْمٌ يَفْرَقُونَ ﴿٥٦﴾

> They swear by Allāh that they are of your number, but they are not of your number. Rather they are people

[20] Allāh, Exalted is He says, *"When you call to prayer they make a mockery and a game of it. That is because they are people who do not use their intellect."* [*al-Mā'idah* (5): 58]

who are scared.

[*at-Tawbah* (9): 56][21]

When Ahlus-Sunnah meet with easy times, aid and victory, hard does it bear down on them and depressed do they become; and when Ahlus-Sunnah meet with straitened times and are tried by Allāh so that their sins may be expiated, jubilant do they become and exultant. This is their legacy and in no way do those who inherit from the Messenger (ﷺ) compare to those who inherit from the hypocrites,

﴿٤٩﴾ إِن تُصِبْكَ حَسَنَةٌ تَسُؤْهُمْ ۖ وَإِن تُصِبْكَ
مُصِيبَةٌ يَقُولُوا قَدْ أَخَذْنَا أَمْرَنَا مِن قَبْلُ وَيَتَوَلَّوا
وَّهُمْ فَرِحُونَ ﴿٥٠﴾ قُل لَّن يُصِيبَنَا إِلَّا مَا كَتَبَ
اللَّهُ لَنَا هُوَ مَوْلَانَا ۚ وَعَلَى اللَّهِ فَلْيَتَوَكَّلِ الْمُؤْمِنُونَ

If good happens to you it galls them. If a mishap occurs to you, they say, 'We made our preparations in advance,' and they turn away rejoicing. Say, 'Nothing can happen to us except what Allāh has ordained for us. He is Our Master and it is in Allāh that the believers should put their trust.'

[*at-Tawbah* (9): 50-51]

إِن تَمْسَسْكُمْ حَسَنَةٌ تَسُؤْهُمْ وَإِن تُصِبْكُمْ سَيِّئَةٌ يَفْرَحُوا
بِهَا ۖ وَإِن تَصْبِرُوا وَتَتَّقُوا لَا يَضُرُّكُمْ كَيْدُهُمْ شَيْئًا ۗ
إِنَّ اللَّهَ بِمَا يَعْمَلُونَ مُحِيطٌ ﴿١٢٠﴾

[21] The next verse reads, *"If they could find a bolt-hole, cave or burrow, they would turn and scurry away into it."* [*at-Tawbah* (9): 57]

> If something good happens to you, it galls them. If something bad strikes you, they rejoice at it. But if you are patient and have taqwā, their scheming will not harm you in any way. Allāh encompasses what they do.
>
> [™*li `Imrān* (3): 120]

Allāh abhors their obeying Him because of the filth of their hearts and impure intentions; as such He held them back and impeded them from obeying Him. He hates to have them close to Him and in His vicinity due to their love of His enemies; as such He distanced them and discarded them. They turned away from His revelation so He turned away from them and decreed misery for them. He judged them with pure justice and they have no hope for victory unless they become of the penitent,[22]

وَلَوْ أَرَادُوا۟ ٱلْخُرُوجَ
لَأَعَدُّوا۟ لَهُۥ عُدَّةً وَلَـٰكِن كَرِهَ ٱللَّهُ ٱنۢبِعَاثَهُمْ فَثَبَّطَهُمْ
وَقِيلَ ٱقْعُدُوا۟ مَعَ ٱلْقَـٰعِدِينَ ﴿٤٦﴾

> If they had really desired to go out, they would have made proper preparations for it, but Allāh was averse to their setting out so he held them back and they were told: 'Stay behind with those who stay behind.'
>
> [*at-Tawbah* (9): 46]

Then He mentions the wisdom behind His doing what has previously been mentioned, He is the Wisest of the wise,

[22] Allāh, Exalted is He says, *"The hypocrites are in the lowest level of Hell and you will not find anyone to help them. Except those who repent and put things right and hold fast to Allāh and dedicate their religion to Allāh Alone."* [*an-Nisā'* (4): 145-146]

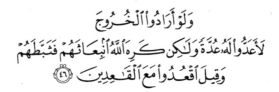

لَوْ خَرَجُوا۟ فِيكُم
مَّا زَادُوكُمْ إِلَّا خَبَالًا وَلَأَوْضَعُوا۟ خِلَٰلَكُمْ يَبْغُونَكُمُ
ٱلْفِتْنَةَ وَفِيكُمْ سَمَّٰعُونَ لَهُمْ ۗ وَٱللَّهُ عَلِيمٌۢ بِٱلظَّٰلِمِينَ ﴿٤٧﴾

> If they had gone out among you, they would have added nothing to you but confusion. They would have scurried about amongst you seeking to cause conflict between you, and among you there were some who would have listened to them. Allāh knows the wrong-doers.
>
> [*at-Tawbah* (9): 47][23]

The texts of the revelation bore down heavily on them so they found them abhorrent, and unable to carry them they renounced them. They were unable to preserve the Sunnah so they ignored it. They found the texts of the Book and Sunnah combating their desires so they laid down laws and principles by which they could reject them or weaken them. Allāh has unveiled their secrets and propounded parables for them. Know that each generation that succeeds them is like them and so He has described them for His friends that they may be aware of them. He says,

ذَٰلِكَ بِأَنَّهُمْ كَرِهُوا۟ مَآ أَنزَلَ ٱللَّهُ فَأَحْبَطَ أَعْمَٰلَهُمْ ﴿٩﴾

> That is because they hate what Allāh has sent down, so He has made their actions come to nothing.
>
> [*Muḥammad* (47): 9]

---

[23] Allāh, Exalted is He, mentions one such example of how some listened to the hypocrites, *"How is it that you have become two parties regarding the hypocrites, when Allāh has returned them to disbelief for what they did? Do you desire to guide people Allāh has misguided?"* [*an-Nisā'* (4): 88]

This holds true for all who find the texts burdensome and see them coming between him and his innovations and desires; its seems to him that he has come across an unbreakable solid structure, so he trades them for false rhetoric, exchanging reality for illusion. This leading to the corruption of his inner and outer,

ذَٰلِكَ بِأَنَّهُمْ قَالُوا لِلَّذِينَ كَرِهُوا مَا نَزَّلَ
ٱللَّهُ سَنُطِيعُكُمْ فِى بَعْضِ ٱلْأَمْرِ وَٱللَّهُ يَعْلَمُ إِسْرَارَهُمْ
﴿٢٦﴾ فَكَيْفَ إِذَا تَوَفَّتْهُمُ ٱلْمَلَٰئِكَةُ يَضْرِبُونَ وُجُوهَهُمْ
وَأَدْبَٰرَهُمْ ﴿٢٧﴾ ذَٰلِكَ بِأَنَّهُمُ ٱتَّبَعُوا مَا أَسْخَطَ ٱللَّهَ
وَكَرِهُوا رِضْوَٰنَهُ فَأَحْبَطَ أَعْمَٰلَهُمْ ﴿٢٨﴾

That is because they said to those who hate what Allāh has sent down, 'We will obey you in part of the affair.' But Allāh knows their secrets. How will it be when the angels take then in death, beating their faces and their backs? That is because they followed what angers Allāh and hated what pleases Him. So He made their actions come to nothing.

[*Muḥammad* (47): 26-28]

They think that if they hide their disbelief and display their faith they will have acquired a great profit, but how can this be so when the All-Seeing has unveiled their secrets?

أَمْ حَسِبَ
ٱلَّذِينَ فِى قُلُوبِهِم مَّرَضٌ أَن لَّن يُخْرِجَ ٱللَّهُ أَضْغَٰنَهُمْ ﴿٢٩﴾
وَلَوْ نَشَاءُ لَأَرَيْنَٰكَهُمْ فَلَعَرَفْتَهُم بِسِيمَٰهُمْ وَلَتَعْرِفَنَّهُمْ فِى
لَحْنِ ٱلْقَوْلِ وَٱللَّهُ يَعْلَمُ أَعْمَٰلَكُمْ ﴿٣٠﴾

> Or did those with sickness in their hearts imagine that Allāh would not expose their malevolence? If We wished, we would show them to you and you would know them by their mark and know them by their ambivalent speech. Allāh knows your actions.
>
> [*Muḥammad* (47): 29-30]

How will they be when they are gathered on the Day of at-Talāq, and Allāh, Mighty and Magnificent, manifests Himself and uncovers His shin? The Day when they are called to prostrate but are unable,

خَٰشِعَةً أَبْصَٰرُهُمْ تَرْهَقُهُمْ ذِلَّةٌ ۖ وَقَدْ كَانُوا۟ يُدْعَوْنَ إِلَى ٱلسُّجُودِ وَهُمْ سَٰلِمُونَ

> Their eyes will be downcast, darkened by debasement; for they were called to prostrate when they were in full possession of their faculties.
>
> [*Qalam* (68): 43]

How will they be when they are gathered together to traverse the Bridge spanning Hell? A bridge finer than a blade of hair and sharper than the edge of a sword, easy to slip off, entrenched in darkness and none can cross it save those guided by a light that shows them where to place their feet. Light is apportioned amongst man, the intensity of light each person has governs the swiftness by which he will cross that bridge. They are given a superficial light with which they accompany the Muslims, just as they used to accompany the Muslims in this life: outwardly praying, giving wealth-tax, performing the pilgrimage, and fasting. When they reach the middle of the bridge their light is blown out by the sharp wind of hypocrisy and they come to a halt in utter confusion, not knowing how to proceed. A wall containing a door is placed between them and the believers, the believers - side of which contains mercy, while the side upon which they find themselves in contains punishment. They cry out to the believers, who in the distance sparkle like stars,

انظُرُونَا نَقْتَبِسْ مِن نُّورِكُمْ

Wait for us so that we can borrow some of your light.
[*al-Ḥadīd* (57): 13]

so that we may cross this bridge in safety,

قِيلَ ارْجِعُوا وَرَاءَكُمْ فَالْتَمِسُوا نُورًا

They will be told, 'Go back and look for light!'
[*al-Ḥadīd* (57): 13]

go back to where the light was first apportioned. Never will any one stop to aid them in such a situation! None will assist another on that path, and a close friend will not turn to aid his friend. They will remind the believers that they accompanied them in this life, just as a wayfarer reminds the resident that he accompanied him on his journey,

أَلَمْ نَكُن مَّعَكُمْ

Were we not with you?
[*al-Ḥadīd* (57): 14]

we fasted with you, prayed with you, recited the Qur'ān with you, and performed the pilgrimage with you; why have we been separated from you! They will reply, your bodies were with us but your hearts were with every deviant and every disbelieving tyrant,

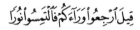

يُنَادُونَهُمْ أَلَمْ نَكُن مَّعَكُمْ ۖ قَالُوا۟ بَلَىٰ وَلَٰكِنَّكُمْ فَتَنتُمْ
أَنفُسَكُمْ وَتَرَبَّصْتُمْ وَٱرْتَبْتُمْ وَغَرَّتْكُمُ ٱلْأَمَانِىُّ حَتَّىٰ جَآءَ أَمْرُ
ٱللَّهِ وَغَرَّكُم بِٱللَّهِ ٱلْغَرُورُ ﴿١٤﴾ فَٱلْيَوْمَ لَا يُؤْخَذُ مِنكُمْ فِدْيَةٌ وَلَا
مِنَ ٱلَّذِينَ كَفَرُوا۟ ۚ مَأْوَىٰكُمُ ٱلنَّارُ ۖ هِىَ مَوْلَىٰكُمْ ۖ وَبِئْسَ ٱلْمَصِيرُ

> But you made trouble for yourselves and hung back and doubted and false hopes deluded you until Allāh's command arrived. The Deluder deluded you about Allāh. So today no ransom will be accepted from you or from those who were disbelievers. Your refuge is the Fire, it is your master. What an evil destination.
>
> [*al-Ḥadīd* (57): 14-15]

The descriptions of these people are numerous; by Allāh what we have omitted is more than we have mentioned. One could almost say that the whole Qur'ān is about them due to their plenitude on the face of this earth and in its belly, namely their graves. There is not a single place on earth except that they are to be found therein. Ḥudhayfah once heard a person saying, 'O Allāh, destroy the hypocrites!' He said, 'Son of my brother, were He to destroy the hypocrites you would find yourself walking down roads alone, because hardly anybody would be left!'

By Allāh, the hearts of the Righteous predecessors lived in dread of hypocrisy because they knew its major and minor manifestations, they knew is generalities and its details and they thought little of themselves to the point that they feared being one of the hypocrites. 'Umar bin al-Khaṭṭāb said to Ḥudhayfah, 'I ask you by Allāh, did the Messenger of Allāh (ﷺ) count me as one of them?' He replied, 'No, and I will not answer this question for any other after you.' Ibn Abī Mulaykah said, 'I met thirty Companions of Muḥammad (ﷺ) and found all of them fearing hypocrisy for himself, and not one of them said that his faith was like the faith of Jibrīl and Mīkā'īl,' (recorded by Bukhārī).

He also recorded that al-Ḥasan al-Baṣrī said, 'None feels safe from hypocrisy except a hypocrite, and none fears it save a believer.' One of the Companions supplicated thus, 'Allāh, I take refuge with you from hypocritical submissiveness.' When asked what it was he replied, 'That the body be seen to be submissive but the heart is not.'

By Allāh, their hearts were overflowing with faith and certainty yet their fear of hypocrisy was great. The faith of many people does not even begin to compare to theirs, yet they claim that their faith is like that of Jibrīl and Mīkā'īl!

The plant of hypocrisy grows from two stems: lying and ostentation. It grows out of two sources: weakness of spiritual insight and weakness of resolution. When these four factors exist, the plant of hypocrisy flourishes and grows firm. However, it grows by the side of waters on the brink of a crumbling precipice, so when they see the flood of reality on the Day when all secrets are disclosed, and the graves are emptied out, and the heart's contents are brought to light, the one whose capital was hypocrisy will discover that all he attained was a mirage,

وَٱلَّذِينَ كَفَرُوٓا۟ أَعْمَٰلُهُمْ كَسَرَابٍۭ
بِقِيعَةٍ يَحْسَبُهُ ٱلظَّمْـَٔانُ مَآءً حَتَّىٰٓ إِذَا جَآءَهُۥ لَمْ يَجِدْهُ شَيْـًٔا
وَوَجَدَ ٱللَّهَ عِندَهُۥ فَوَفَّىٰهُ حِسَابَهُۥ ۗ وَٱللَّهُ سَرِيعُ ٱلْحِسَابِ ﴿٣٩﴾

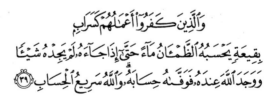

> A thirsty man thinks it is water but when he reaches it, he finds it to be nothing at all, but he finds Allāh there. He will pay him his accounts in full. Allāh is swift at reckoning.
>
> [*an-Nūr* (24): 39]

Their hearts are heedless of performing good but their bodies outwardly do so, and indecent deeds are frequently performed by them. When they hear the truth their hearts are too hard to accept it, but when they witness falsehood and hear fallacy, their hearts openly accept it and they lend a willing ear.

By Allāh, these are the signs of hypocrisy, so beware of them! Beware of them before the judgment comes upon you: when they are entrusted with something they break the trust, when they promise they break it, when they speak they are not fair and just, when they are called to obedience they falter, when they are called to what Allāh has revealed and to His Messenger they turn away, but when it suits their whims and desires they rush to it. Leave them to the subjugation and misery they have chosen for themselves, rely not on their contracts and trust not in their promises for they are liars,

وَمِنْهُم مَّنْ عَٰهَدَ ٱللَّهَ لَئِنْ
ءَاتَىٰنَا مِن فَضْلِهِۦ لَنَصَّدَّقَنَّ وَلَنَكُونَنَّ مِنَ ٱلصَّٰلِحِينَ ﴿٧٥﴾
فَلَمَّآ ءَاتَىٰهُم مِّن فَضْلِهِۦ بَخِلُوا۟ بِهِۦ وَتَوَلَّوا۟ وَّهُم مُّعْرِضُونَ
﴿٧٦﴾ فَأَعْقَبَهُمْ نِفَاقًا فِى قُلُوبِهِمْ إِلَىٰ يَوْمِ يَلْقَوْنَهُۥ بِمَآ أَخْلَفُوا۟
ٱللَّهَ مَا وَعَدُوهُ وَبِمَا كَانُوا۟ يَكْذِبُونَ ﴿٧٧﴾

> Among them were some who made an agreement with Allāh: 'If He gives us of His bounty we will definitely

> give in charity and be among the righteous.' But when He does give them of His bounty they are tight-fisted with it and turn away, so he has punished them by putting hypocrisy in their hearts until the Day they meet Him because they failed Allāh in what they promised Him and because they lied.
>
> [*at-Tawbah* (9): 75-77]

Peace and Blessings be upon our Prophet, Muḥammad, his family and his Companions.[24]

---

[24] ibn al-Qayyim, *Madārij as-Sālikīn* [1/376-389].

APPENDIX ONE

The Parable of the Hypocrites

Imām ibn Qayyim al-Jawziyyah
may Allāh have mercy upon him

APPENDIX ONE

The Parable of the Hypocrites Ibn al-Qayyim on *al-Baqarah* (2): 17-20

Allāh, Exalted is He, says in *Sūrah al-Baqarah* concerning the hypocrites:

مَثَلُهُمْ كَمَثَلِ ٱلَّذِى ٱسْتَوْقَدَ نَارًا فَلَمَّآ أَضَآءَتْ مَا حَوْلَهُۥ
ذَهَبَ ٱللَّهُ بِنُورِهِمْ وَتَرَكَهُمْ فِى ظُلُمَٰتٍ لَّا يُبْصِرُونَ ﴿١٧﴾ صُمٌّۢ
بُكْمٌ عُمْىٌ فَهُمْ لَا يَرْجِعُونَ ﴿١٨﴾ أَوْ كَصَيِّبٍ مِّنَ ٱلسَّمَآءِ فِيهِ
ظُلُمَٰتٌ وَرَعْدٌ وَبَرْقٌ يَجْعَلُونَ أَصَٰبِعَهُمْ فِىٓ ءَاذَانِهِم مِّنَ ٱلصَّوَٰعِقِ
حَذَرَ ٱلْمَوْتِ ۚ وَٱللَّهُ مُحِيطٌۢ بِٱلْكَٰفِرِينَ ﴿١٩﴾ يَكَادُ ٱلْبَرْقُ يَخْطَفُ
أَبْصَٰرَهُمْ ۖ كُلَّمَآ أَضَآءَ لَهُم مَّشَوْا۟ فِيهِ وَإِذَآ أَظْلَمَ عَلَيْهِمْ قَامُوا۟ ۚ
وَلَوْ شَآءَ ٱللَّهُ لَذَهَبَ بِسَمْعِهِمْ وَأَبْصَٰرِهِمْ ۚ إِنَّ ٱللَّهَ عَلَىٰ كُلِّ
شَىْءٍ قَدِيرٌ ﴿٢٠﴾

17. Their likeness is that of one who kindled a fire, and then when it had lit up all around them, Allāh re-

moved their light and left them in darknesses, unable to see.

18. Deaf, dumb and blind, they will not return.
19. Or that of a storm-cloud in the sky, full of darkness, thunder and lightning. They thrust their fingers in their ears against the thunderclaps, fearful of death. Allāh encompasses the disbelievers.
20. The lightning all but snatches away their sight. Whenever they have light, they walk therein but whenever darkness covers them, they halt. If Allāh wished, He could take away their hearing and their sight; for Allāh has power over all things.

Allāh, Glorious is He, has propounded a parable for His enemies, the hypocrites, with a people who ignited a fire in order to acquire light and benefit - for they were a people on a journey who had lost their way. When this fire had alighted and lit up their surroundings, they were able to see the right path, they were able to see what would benefit them and what would harm them; but then, suddenly, the light was extinguished and they were left in darkness: all three routes to guidance were barred them. *'Deaf, dumb and blind,'* guidance comes to a servant from three doors: what he hears with his ears; what he sees with his eyes; and what he understands with his heart; these people's hearts are unable to comprehend, they cannot see, and neither can they hear.[1] It is

[1] Ibn al-Qayyim, *Miftāḥ Dār as-Sa'ādah* [1/245-256] said, 'Allāh, Glorious is He, has described the denizens of the Fire as being people of ignorance, and He informed us that the routes to knowledge have been barred to them. He said, *"They will say, 'If only we had listened and used our intellect, we not have been denizens of the Blaze.'"* [*al-Mulk* (67): 10-11] Hearing and intellect are the foundations of knowledge and by them does one acquire it, *"We have created many of the jinn and men for Hell. They have hearts they do not understand with. They have ears they do not hear*

=

also said that because they gained no benefit from their ears, sight, and hearts; they were as good as those who had no faculty of hearing, seeing, and comprehension; and hence were described as such. Both these opinions are of the same meaning and go hand-in-hand. *'They will not return,'* in the light they had seen the path of guidance, but when the light left them, they did not return to that guidance.

Allāh, Glorious and Exalted is He said, *'Allāh removed their light,'* placing the particle *'ba'* before the word *'light,'*[2] and there is a notable reason for this. That is that this usage serves to show that Allāh has removed from them His special closeness that is reserved for the believers only. Therefore, after His removing their light, He neither stays 'close' to them or 'with' them. They have no place in His sayings,

لَا تَحْزَنْ إِنَّ ٱللَّهَ مَعَنَا ۖ

Do not be despondent, Allāh is with us.
[*at-Tawbah* (9): 40]

قَالَ كَلَّآ ۖ إِنَّ مَعِيَ رَبِّي سَيَهْدِينِ ﴿٦٢﴾

=
with. They have eyes they do not see with. Such people are like cattle, rather they are even further astray! They are the unaware." [*al-A'rāf* (7): 179] Here, He informs us that they have not acquired knowledge from any of its three doors: intellect, hearing, and seeing... *"Deaf - dumb - blind. They do no use their intellect."* [*al-Baqarah* (2): 171] Allāh, Exalted is He says, *"Have they not travelled about the earth and do they not have hearts to understand with or ears to hear with? It is not their eyes which are blind but the hearts in their breasts which are blind."* [*al-Ḥajj* (22): 46], *"We gave them hearing, sight, and hearts. But their hearing, sight, and hearts were of no use to them at all when they renounced Allāh's signs and what they mocked at engulfed them."* [*al-Aḥqāf* (46): 26]'

[2] Saying, *'bi nūrihim,'* as opposed to *'nūrahum.'*

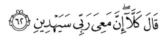

> He said, 'Never! My Lord is with me and He will guide me.'
>
> [*ash-Shu'arā'* (26): 62]

Ponder carefully His saying, *'then when it had lit up all around them,'* how this light is clearly shown to be distinct and separate from them, for had it been a light that was intrinsic to them, it would not have left them. Therefore it was a light that surrounded them but did not enter them, it was something fleeting whereas the darkness was something permanent and intrinsic to them. Hence the light returned to its source and the darkness remained in its source, all of this was done as a proof from Allāh and for an all-encompassing wisdom that none but those endowed with understanding can see.

Ponder carefully His saying, *'Allāh removed their light,'* how He did not say, 'Allāh removed their fire,' such that the wording would conform to that found at the beginning of this verse. Why is this? Fire has both the property to give light and the property to burn, so its property of light was removed leaving only the property to burn and harm.[3]

Ponder carefully His saying *'their light'* how He did not say 'their glow (*ḍaw'*),' despite the fact that He said, *'then when it had lit up all*

---

[3] Ibn al-Qayyim explains this further in his *Wābil as-Ṣayyib*, translated as *The Invocation of God* [p. 67], 'Such is the state of the hypocrites. The light of their faith has been removed by hypocrisy, leaving to smoulder in their hearts the heat of disbelief, doubts, and questionable practices. And as heat and flames singe their hearts in this world, so, too, on the Day of Judgment will God place them in a *'kindled Fire that reaches up to the hearts.'* Such is the similitude of one who no longer goes through this world by the light of faith, who abandons it and removes himself from it after it had lit his way.

around them,' employing the words *ḍawʾ*. The word *ḍawʾ* refers, essentially, to that light which is extraneous to basic light. So if Allāh had said that He had taken away their *ḍawʾ* it would have suggested that only the extraneous light had been taken away and not the basic light. Now because light, *nūr*, is the basis upon which *ḍawʾ* is built, to say that the *nūr* has been taken away automatically presupposes that the *ḍawʾ* has also been taken away. This then stresses the fact that they are people of darkness and have no light in any of its forms: the Book which Allāh has called light; the Messenger (ﷺ) which Allāh has called light; His religion which Allāh has called light; His guidance which Allāh has called light; one of His Names is 'the Light'; and the prayer which is light. Allāh's taking away their light means that He took all this away from them.

Ponder carefully how this parable completely corresponds to the previously given parable,

أُولَٰٓئِكَ ٱلَّذِينَ ٱشۡتَرَوُاْ ٱلضَّلَٰلَةَ
بِٱلۡهُدَىٰ فَمَا رَبِحَت تِّجَٰرَتُهُمۡ وَمَا كَانُواْ مُهۡتَدِينَ ﴿١٦﴾

> Those are the people who have sold guidance for misguidance. Their trade has brought them no profit and they are not guided.
>
> [*al-Baqarah* (2): 16]

how they acquired this misguidance at the expense of guidance, giving it away happily;[4] and here how they happily acquired dark-

---

[4] A person enters a transaction of his own free will and is free to buy, or not buy, the commodity. The fact that these people, without coercion, bought misguidance shows that they were happy with it. This is why the author makes a point of mentioning the fact that they happily bought it. Allāh knows best.

ness - misguidance - at the expense of light - guidance. Hence they have sold light and guidance and bought darkness and misguidance... what a wretched transaction!

Ponder carefully how Allāh says, *'Allāh removed their light,'* but says, *'and left them in darknesses,'* mentioning light in the singular and darkness in the plural. The truth is one, and that is Allāh's Straight Path: the only path that leads to Him: worshipping Allāh Alone in accordance to what has been legislated upon the tongue of His Messenger (ﷺ); not with ones own desires and innovations. However the ways of falsehood are many and this is why Allāh mentions the truth in its singular form but falsehood in its plural,

ٱللَّهُ وَلِيُّ ٱلَّذِينَ ءَامَنُوا۟ يُخْرِجُهُم مِّنَ ٱلظُّلُمَٰتِ إِلَى ٱلنُّورِ ۖ
وَٱلَّذِينَ كَفَرُوٓا۟ أَوْلِيَآؤُهُمُ ٱلطَّٰغُوتُ يُخْرِجُونَهُم مِّنَ
ٱلنُّورِ إِلَى ٱلظُّلُمَٰتِ ۗ أُو۟لَٰٓئِكَ أَصْحَٰبُ ٱلنَّارِ ۖ هُمْ فِيهَا
خَٰلِدُونَ ﴿٢٥٧﴾

> Allāh is the protector of those who believe. He brings them out of the darknesses into the light. But the disbelievers have false gods as protectors, they take them from the light into the darknesses...
>
> [*al-Baqarah* (2): 257]

وَأَنَّ هَٰذَا صِرَٰطِى مُسْتَقِيمًا فَٱتَّبِعُوهُ ۖ وَلَا تَتَّبِعُوا۟ ٱلسُّبُلَ
فَتَفَرَّقَ بِكُمْ عَن سَبِيلِهِۦ ۚ ذَٰلِكُمْ وَصَّىٰكُم بِهِۦ لَعَلَّكُمْ
تَتَّقُونَ ﴿١٥٣﴾

> This is My Path and it is straight, so follow it. Do not follow other ways or you will become cut off from His Way. That is what He instructs you to do so that hopefully you will have taqwā.
>
> [*al-Anʿām* (6): 153]

This does not contradict His saying,

يَهۡدِي بِهِ ٱللَّهُ مَنِ ٱتَّبَعَ رِضۡوَٰنَهُۥ سُبُلَ
ٱلسَّلَٰمِ

> By it, Allāh guides those who follow what pleases Him to the ways of Peace.
>
> [*al-Mā'idah* (5): 16]

for this verse makes reference to the ways and routes that can be taken to please Him, all of which are contained within His one path, the Straight Path. It is authentically reported that the Prophet (ﷺ) drew a straight line on the ground and said, 'This is the path of Allāh,' then he drew lines to the left and right of this line and said, 'These are the other paths, at the head of every path is a devil calling to it,' then he recited the verse,

وَأَنَّ هَٰذَا صِرَٰطِي مُسۡتَقِيمٗا فَٱتَّبِعُوهُۖ وَلَا تَتَّبِعُواْ ٱلسُّبُلَ
فَتَفَرَّقَ بِكُمۡ عَن سَبِيلِهِۦۚ ذَٰلِكُمۡ وَصَّىٰكُم بِهِۦ لَعَلَّكُمۡ
تَتَّقُونَ ﴿١٥٣﴾

> This is My Path and it is straight, so follow it. Do not follow other ways or you will become cut off from His Way. That is what He instructs you to do so that hopefully you will have taqwā.

[*al-An'ām* (6): 153][5]

It is also said in explanation to this first parable that it is a similitude for what the hypocrites kindle of the fire of trial and tribulation that they seek to covertly spread amongst the Muslims, as such it would be in the same vein as His saying,

كُلَّمَآ أَوْقَدُوا۟ نَارًا لِّلْحَرْبِ أَطْفَأَهَا ٱللَّهُ

Each time they kindle the fire of war, Allāh extinguishes it.

[*al-Mā'idah* (5): 64]

So, *'Allāh removed their light'* would have the same meaning as, *'Allāh extinguishes it'*; the foiling of their efforts and the falsification of their claims would have the same meaning as leaving them in darkness and confusion: deaf, dumb, and blind.

It is problematic that this latter explanation be the correct exegesis to this verse, even though it, in and of itself is true. The context does not lend itself to this explanation. The one who kindles the fire of war does not have light that surrounds him, and the one who kindles the fire of war has no light that could be taken from him. The fact that they have been left in darkness, unable to see, means that they moved from a state in which they could see knowledge and guidance to a state of doubt and disbelief, not that they kindled the fire of war.

Al-Ḥasan said, 'It refers to the hypocrite: he saw, then became blind; he knew, then rejected.' This is why He says, *'they will not*

[5] Aḥmad on the authority of ibn Mas'ūd.

return,' i.e. they will not return to the light that they left. Allāh says with regards the disbelievers,

صُمٌّۢ بُكۡمٌ عُمۡيٞ فَهُمۡ لَا يَعۡقِلُونَ

Deaf - dumb - blind. They do not use their intellect.
[*al-Baqarah* (2): 171]

and thereby negated comprehension from them as they are not people of faith and insight, not having entered Islām. But with regards the hypocrites, He negated the fact that they would return because they had believed, then disbelieved, and would not return to faith.

Then after propounding this parable of fire, Allāh propounds another parable for the hypocrites, this time of water. *Ṣayyib* mentioned in the verse refers to driving rain which pours down from the sky. Here the guidance with which He guided His servants has been likened to water because guidance gives life to the hearts as water gives life to the earth. The portion that the hypocrite gets from this guidance is the same as one who is caught in this storm-cloud but gets nothing from it save darkness, thunder, and lightning; having no notion of its many benefits such as life for the earth - its animals and vegetation - springs forth after rain. The darkness, thunder, and lightning in a storm-cloud are not matters that are desired in and of themselves, rather they are matters that lead to the accomplishment of what is desired from this cloud. The ignoramus suffices with merely seeing the outward effects of this cloud: the darkness, the thunder, the lightning, the cold, and the fact that he is prevented from travelling; but has no inkling of the huge benefit that comes as a result of this rain. This is true of every short-sighted, dull witted person; his perception does not go deeper than seeing the outward form of things and he does not what is behind them. This is the state of the majority of creation except for a few amongst them. When the short-sighted sees the hardship and toil that is to be found in Jihād, when he sees the fact that he could be wounded, censured by certain people, and excite the enmity of others; he does not go forth for Jihād. He is unable to probe deeper and realise the great benefits, the praiseworthy goals, and great rewards it contains. When one of them desires to perform the pilgrimage and sees the hardships entailed in the journey, the leaving of the comfort of his home and town, and the difficulties to be faced, he cannot see beyond this to what lies at the end of this journey and as such falters and does not undertake it.

This is the state of those who lack spiritual insight and are weak of faith: those who see the threats, promises, commands, and prohibitions that are to be found in the Qur'ān as ordinances that are too heavy for their egos which desire only to follow their lusts. These ordinances wean the soul of its base qualities. Weaning is truly difficult for the child; and all men are children with respect to their intellects with the exception of those who have weaned and regulated them, and as such have comprehended the truth by way of knowledge and action. It is such people who are able to see what is behind this storm-cloud; what is behind the darkness, thunder, and lightning; it is such people who realise that this storm-cloud is the source of life for existence.

Az-Zamakhsharī said, 'The religion of Islām has been likened to the cloud, because hearts are given life by it as the earth is by water; disbelief has been likened to darkness; threat and promise has been likened to thunder and lightning; and trials and tribulations that terrify the disbelievers have been likened to thunderclaps. The meaning of *'or that of a storm-cloud'* is 'or that of people caught in a storm-cloud.'

Both these parables contain great points of wisdom:

i) The one who is seeking light is seeking light from something else, not from himself; when that light goes, he remains in that original darkness. This is the state of the hypocrite; he affirms belief on his tongue but does not believe or have love in his heart; as such what light he acquires as a result of this is borrowed.

ii) Fire requires fuel to keep it alight. This fuel is comparable to food that is required to sustain animal life. Likewise the light of faith requires fuel so as to maintain it: beneficial knowledge and righteous action. If this fuel is taken away, it dies out.

iii) Darkness is of two types: a perpetual darkness which is not preceded by light and a temporal darkness which is preceded by light. It is the latter of these two which is most severe upon the one who faces it. The darkness of the disbelievers is of the first type for they have never seen the light, the darkness of the hypocrites is of the second type for they saw the light and then were plunged in darkness.

iv) This parable points to their state in the Hereafter for there they will be given a superficial light just as their light in this world was superficial. Then, at the time when they need light most, it will suddenly die: they will halt on the Bridge and be unable to cross it for only those with firm

> light may do so. That light is only made firm with beneficial knowledge and righteous actions. Therefore their parable which describes their state in this life corresponds to their state in the Hereafter: when light is apportioned to the people before the Bridge, the light of the believers will remain and the light of the hypocrites will die. When this is understood one understands why Allāh said, *'Allāh removed their light,'* employing the *'bā'* and did not say *'adhhabaAllāhu Nūrahum.'*

For further detail one can read the ḥadīth recorded by Muslim on the authority of Jābir bin 'Abdullāh (*raḍiyAllāhu 'anhumā*). He was asked about the crossing of the Bridge to which he replied, "We would come on the Day of Judgement on a hill standing above the people. Then the people will be summoned along with the idols that they used to worship, one after another. Then our Lord, Blessed and Exalted, would come to us and say, 'Who are you waiting for?' They would say, 'We are waiting for our Lord.' He would say, 'I am your Lord.' They say, 'We are not sure until we look upon You.' He would then manifest Himself and laugh, and would leave with them following. Every person among them, the believer and hypocrite, would be given light. On the Bridge spanning Hell there would be hooks and spikes which would take whoever Allāh willed. Then the light of the hypocrites would die out and the believers would secure salvation. The first group saved would consist of seventy thousand people whose faces would be like the moon and they will not be judged. The next group would have faces like the stars of the sky, and so on. The intercession would commence till the point that there would come out of Hellfire the one who said, 'None has the right to be worshipped save Allāh,' and there was only in his heart a barley grain's worth of faith. They would be brought to the courtyard of Paradise and the inhabitants of Paradise would sprinkle water over them...," to the end of the ḥadīth.

Ponder carefully his saying, '...and would leave with them following. Every person among them, the believer and hypocrite, would be given light...,' and ponder carefully His saying, *'Allāh removed their light and left them in darknesses, unable to see,'* and ponder their state when their light is extinguished and they are left in the pitch of darkness whereas the believers proceed on, following their Lord. Ponder his (ﷺ) saying in the ḥadīth concerning the intercession, 'Every nation will follow the god that they used to worship,' the polytheist will follow his god and the person of *Tawḥīd* will follow Allāh. Ponder His saying,

يَوْمَ يُكْشَفُ عَن سَاقٍ وَيُدْعَوْنَ إِلَى ٱلسُّجُودِ فَلَا يَسْتَطِيعُونَ ﴿٤٢﴾

> The Day the shin will be uncovered and they are summoned to prostrate but they will not be able to.
>
> [*al-Qalam* (68): 42]

He (ﷺ) mentioned this verse in the ḥadīth of intercession on this occasion talked about in the previous ḥadīth and in the ḥadīth he said, '...so He will uncover His shin,' and thereby made clear that it was His shin that was being talked about in the verse. Ponder all of this and you will come to understand a secret from the secrets of *Tawḥīd*, understanding of the Qur'ān, and how Allāh deals with the people of *Tawḥīd* as compared to the people of *shirk*.

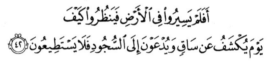

v) The first parable deals with them acquiring darkness which is a similitude for misguidance and confusion, the opposite of which is guidance. The second parable deals with their acquiring fear, the opposite of which is safety and security. The hypocrites are not guided and neither are they safe,

ٱلَّذِينَ ءَامَنُواْ وَلَمْ يَلْبِسُوٓاْ إِيمَـٰنَهُم بِظُلْمٍ أُوْلَـٰٓئِكَ لَهُمُ ٱلْأَمْنُ وَهُم مُّهْتَدُونَ ﴿٨٢﴾

> Those who believe and do not mix their faith with any wrongdoing, they are the ones who are safe; it is they who are guided.
>
> [*al-An'ām* (6): 82]

Ibn 'Abbās and other exegetes said, 'The similitude of these people's hypocrisy is that of a person who kindled a fire in a dark night on a terrifying occasion. He warms himself up, sees what is around him, and is saved from what he feared; then while in that state, the fire is suddenly extinguished and he remains once again in that darkness in a state of fear and utter confusion. The hypocrites, by their outwardly testifying to faith, have secured their wealth and children, they marry the believers, they inherit from them, and they acquire a portion of the war booty. This is their light, but when they die, they return once again to darkness and fear.'

Mujāhid said, 'The fire alighting for them means their going towards the Muslims and guidance. Their light being taken away means their going towards the polytheists and misguidance.'

The acquiring of light and its removal has been explained variously to take place in this life, or the life of the grave, or in the

Hereafter. The correct position is that it occurs in all three stages of life, for they are recompensed for their state in this world in all three stages with,

جَزَآءً وِفَاقًا ﴿٢٦﴾

...a fitting recompense.

[*an-Naba'* (78): 26]

وَمَا رَبُّكَ بِظَلَّٰمٍ لِّلْعَبِيدِ ﴿٤٦﴾

Your Lord does not wrong His slaves.

[*Fuṣṣilat* (41): 46]

In the resurrection a person shall reap what he sowed in this world and that is why it is called the Day of Recompense,

وَمَن كَانَ فِي هَٰذِهِۦٓ أَعْمَىٰ فَهُوَ فِي ٱلْأٓخِرَةِ أَعْمَىٰ وَأَضَلُّ سَبِيلًا ﴿٧٢﴾

Those who are blind in this world will be blind in the Hereafter and even further off the Path.

[*al-Isrā'* (17): 72]

وَيَزِيدُ ٱللَّهُ ٱلَّذِينَ ٱهْتَدَوْا۟ هُدًى

Allāh augments those who are guided by giving them greater guidance.

[*Maryam* (19): 76][6]

To return to the discussion at hand...Allāh, the Blessed and Exalted, has propounded two parables, one for fire and one for wa-

[6] At this point the author, may Allāh have mercy upon, digresses to lengthy discussion concerning this issue. Since it is unrelated to the explanation of the parable at hand, the translator has opted to omit it.

ter, in *Sūrah al-Baqarah*, *Sūrah al-Ra'd*, and *Sūrah al-Nūr*. This is because life comes about through water and light; the believer has a living and illuminated heart, and the hypocrite has a dead and dark heart. Allāh, Exalted is He says,

أَوَمَن كَانَ مَيْتًا فَأَحْيَيْنَٰهُ وَجَعَلْنَا لَهُۥ نُورًا يَمْشِي بِهِۦ فِي
ٱلنَّاسِ كَمَن مَّثَلُهُۥ فِي ٱلظُّلُمَٰتِ لَيْسَ بِخَارِجٍ مِّنْهَا

> Is someone who was dead and whom We brought to life, supplying him with light by which to walk among people, the same as someone who is in utter darkness, unable to emerge from it?
>
> [*al-An'ām* (6): 122]

وَمَا يَسْتَوِي ٱلْأَعْمَىٰ وَٱلْبَصِيرُ ﴿١٩﴾ وَلَا ٱلظُّلُمَٰتُ وَلَا ٱلنُّورُ
﴿٢٠﴾ وَلَا ٱلظِّلُّ وَلَا ٱلْحَرُورُ ﴿٢١﴾ وَمَا يَسْتَوِي ٱلْأَحْيَآءُ وَلَا ٱلْأَمْوَٰتُ
إِنَّ ٱللَّهَ يُسْمِعُ مَن يَشَآءُ وَمَآ أَنتَ بِمُسْمِعٍ مَّن فِي ٱلْقُبُورِ ﴿٢٢﴾

> The blind and the seeing are not the same, nor are darkness and light, nor are cool shade and fierce heat. The living and dead are not the same, Allāh makes anyone He wills to hear but you cannot make those in the grave to hear.
>
> [*Fāṭir* (35): 19-22]

Therefore He considered those who follow His guidance, and illuminate themselves with His light to be alive, taking refuge under a shade that saves them from the heat of doubts, misguidance, innovation, and *shirk*. And He considered one who does not do so to be blind and dead, submerged in the heat of disbelief, *shirk* and misguidance, engulfed in layer after layer of darkness.

Allāh knows best.[7]

[7] Ibn Qayyim, *Ijtimā' al-Juyūsh al-Islāmiyyah* [pp. 63-72, 79-87]; *Tafsīr al-Qayyim* [pp.114-126]. The author also has an explanation to both these parables in his *al-Amthāl fi-l Qur'ān* and *al-Wābil al-Ṣayyib.*

APPENDIX TWO

On *al-Baqarah* (2): 19-20

Imām al-Shanqīṭī

may Allāh have mercy upon him

APPENDIX TWO

al-Shanqīṭī on *al-Baqarah* (2): 19-20

Allāh, Exalted is He, says in *Sūrah al-Baqarah* concerning the hypocrites:

أَوْ كَصَيِّبٍ مِّنَ ٱلسَّمَآءِ فِيهِ
ظُلُمَٰتٌ وَرَعْدٌ وَبَرْقٌ يَجْعَلُونَ أَصَٰبِعَهُمْ فِىٓ ءَاذَانِهِم مِّنَ ٱلصَّوَٰعِقِ
حَذَرَ ٱلْمَوْتِ ۚ وَٱللَّهُ مُحِيطٌۢ بِٱلْكَٰفِرِينَ ﴿١٩﴾ يَكَادُ ٱلْبَرْقُ يَخْطَفُ
أَبْصَٰرَهُمْ ۖ كُلَّمَآ أَضَآءَ لَهُم مَّشَوْا۟ فِيهِ وَإِذَآ أَظْلَمَ عَلَيْهِمْ قَامُوا۟ ۚ
وَلَوْ شَآءَ ٱللَّهُ لَذَهَبَ بِسَمْعِهِمْ وَأَبْصَٰرِهِمْ ۚ إِنَّ ٱللَّهَ عَلَىٰ كُلِّ
شَىْءٍ قَدِيرٌ ﴿٢٠﴾

19. Or that of a storm-cloud in the sky, full of darkness, thunder and lightning. They thrust their fingers in their ears against the thunderclaps, fearful of death. Allāh encompasses the disbelievers.
20. The lightning all but snatches away their sight. Whenever they have light, they walk therein but whenever darkness covers them, they halt. If Allāh wished, He could take away their hearing and their sight; for Allāh has power over all things.

The saying of the Exalted, *'Or that of a storm-cloud,' Ṣayyib* means rain. Allāh has set forth a parable in this verse for the guidance and knowledge that the Messenger of Allāh (ﷺ) came with, likening it to rain. It is likened so because knowledge and guidance is a source of life for the souls just as water is a source of life for the bodies. This aspect of the parable was indicated by Allāh in His saying,

وَهُوَ ٱلَّذِى يُرْسِلُ
ٱلرِّيَٰحَ بُشْرًۢا بَيْنَ يَدَىْ رَحْمَتِهِۦ ۖ حَتَّىٰٓ إِذَآ أَقَلَّتْ سَحَابًا
ثِقَالًا سُقْنَٰهُ لِبَلَدٍ مَّيِّتٍ فَأَنزَلْنَا بِهِ ٱلْمَآءَ فَأَخْرَجْنَا بِهِۦ مِن كُلِّ
ٱلثَّمَرَٰتِ ۚ كَذَٰلِكَ نُخْرِجُ ٱلْمَوْتَىٰ لَعَلَّكُمْ تَذَكَّرُونَ ﴿٥٧﴾

> It is He who sends out the winds as heralds of good tidings going before His mercy so that when they have lifted up heavy clouds, We despatch them to a land that is dead and send down water to it...the vegetation of a good land comes forth by the permission of its Lord, but that which is bad only yields scantily.
>
> [*al-A'rāf* (7): 57-58]

The Messenger (ﷺ) explained this aspect of the parable clearly in the hadīth of Abū Mūsā (*raḍiyAllāhu 'anhu*) recorded by Bukhārī and Muslim wherein he (ﷺ) said, 'The similitude of the guidance and knowledge that Allāh has sent me with is like abundant rain falling on the earth; some of which has fertile soil that absorbed the rain water and brought forth vegetation and grass in abundance; and another portion of it was hard and held the rain water and Allāh benefited the people with it and they utilised it for drinking, making their animals drink from it, and for irrigation of the land for cultivation; and a portion of it was barren which could neither hold water nor bring forth vegetation. This similitude betokens the one who understands the religion, benefits from what Allāh has sent me with, learns and teaches it; and the one who pays not heed and does not accept the guidance with which I have been sent.'

'Full of darkness,' Allāh has set forth a parable in this verse regarding the doubts and suspicion that have afflicted the hypocrites with respect to the Qur'ān - comparing these to the darkness in the storm-cloud which in turn has been set forth as a similitude to the Qur'ān. Allāh has illustrated a number of occasions, in other verses, which are like darkness for them because they increase them only in blindness. He says,

وَمَا جَعَلْنَا ٱلْقِبْلَةَ ٱلَّتِى كُنتَ عَلَيْهَآ إِلَّا لِنَعْلَمَ مَن يَتَّبِعُ ٱلرَّسُولَ مِمَّن يَنقَلِبُ عَلَىٰ عَقِبَيْهِ ۚ وَإِن كَانَتْ لَكَبِيرَةً إِلَّا عَلَى ٱلَّذِينَ هَدَى ٱللَّهُ ۗ

> We only appointed the *Qiblah* which you used to face in order to know those who follow the Messenger from those who would turn on their heels. Though in truth it was a very hard thing - except for those Allāh has guided.
>
> [*al-Baqarah* (2):143]

The abrogation of the *Qiblah* from Jerusalem to the Ka'bah made the people having weak conviction think that the Messenger (ﷺ) was not certain of his message: for one day he was facing one direction in prayer and another day another direction! This is why Allāh has said,

سَيَقُولُ ٱلسُّفَهَآءُ مِنَ ٱلنَّاسِ مَا وَلَّىٰهُمْ عَن قِبْلَتِهِمُ ٱلَّتِى كَانُوا۟ عَلَيْهَا ۚ

> The fools among the people will ask, 'What has made them change from the *Qiblah* they used to face?'
>
> [*al-Baqarah* (2):142]

So Allāh has made clear that the abrogation of the *Qiblah* was hard upon those whom Allāh did not guide and strengthen his conviction in His saying, *'Indeed it was a great test except for those whom Allāh guided.'*

Another example lies in His saying,

وَإِذْ قُلْنَا لَكَ إِنَّ رَبَّكَ أَحَاطَ بِٱلنَّاسِ ۚ وَمَا جَعَلْنَا ٱلرُّءْيَا ٱلَّتِىٓ أَرَيْنَٰكَ إِلَّا فِتْنَةً لِّلنَّاسِ وَٱلشَّجَرَةَ ٱلْمَلْعُونَةَ فِى ٱلْقُرْءَانِ ۚ وَنُخَوِّفُهُمْ فَمَا يَزِيدُهُمْ إِلَّا طُغْيَٰنًا كَبِيرًا ﴿٦٠﴾

> We made not the vision which We showed you and the accursed tree in the Qur'ān but a trial for mankind. We warn and frighten them but it increases them only in excessive insolence.
>
> [*al-Isrā'* (17): 60]

What he (ﷺ) was shown on the night of Isrā' and Mi'rāj was from amongst the miracles and wonders bestowed him, therefore it was a means of strengthening the belief of the disbelievers that he (ﷺ) was a liar because they thought that what he was informing them of could not possibly occur. Hence, this event was a means by which the misguided increased in misguidance. Likewise, the accursed tree in the Qur'ān, which is the tree of *Zaqqūm*, was also a means of increasing the misguided in misguidance, for when they heard the Prophet (ﷺ) reciting,

إِنَّهَا شَجَرَةٌ تَخْرُجُ فِي أَصْلِ الْجَحِيمِ ﴿٦٤﴾

> Indeed it is a tree that springs out of the depths of the Blazing Fire,
>
> [*as-Ṣaffāt* (37): 64]

they said, 'His lie has become clear: a tree will not grow in a desert so how can one grow in the bottom of Hellfire!'

Another example lies in His saying,

وَمَا جَعَلْنَا عِدَّتَهُمْ إِلَّا فِتْنَةً لِّلَّذِينَ كَفَرُوا

> We have only specified their number as a trial for the disbelievers,
>
> [*al-Muddaththir* (74): 31]

When he (ﷺ) recited the verse,

عَلَيْهَا تِسْعَةَ عَشَرَ

> There are nineteen in charge of it.
>
> [*al-Muddaththir* (74): 30]

some of the people said, 'This is such a small number guarding this Fire that Muḥammad (ﷺ) thinks that we shall enter that we are capable of killing them and then taking Paradise by force!'

Allāh, Exalted is He, did this as a test for them, and He has an all-encompassing wisdom behind doing so, and He is Exalted, far above what the unbelievers say.

'Thunder,' Allāh has set forth a similitude to thunder due to what the Qur'ān contains of rebukes that ring in the ears and stir the heart, some of which are mentioned in other verses such as His sayings,

فَإِنْ أَعْرَضُوا فَقُلْ أَنذَرْتُكُمْ صَٰعِقَةً

> If they turn away, say: 'I have warned you of a destructive awful cry.'
>
> [*Fuṣṣilat* (41): 13]

يَٰٓأَيُّهَا ٱلَّذِينَ أُوتُوا۟ ٱلْكِتَٰبَ ءَامِنُوا۟ بِمَا نَزَّلْنَا
مُصَدِّقًا لِّمَا مَعَكُم مِّن قَبْلِ أَن نَّطْمِسَ وُجُوهًا فَنَرُدَّهَا
عَلَىٰٓ أَدْبَارِهَآ أَوْ نَلْعَنَهُمْ

> You who have been given the Book! Believe in what We have revealed confirming what is already with you, before We obliterate faces, turning them inside out, or We curse them...
>
> [*an-Nisā'* (4): 47]

إِلَّا نَذِيرٌ لَّكُم بَيْنَ يَدَىْ عَذَابٍ شَدِيدٍ ﴿٤٦﴾

> He is only a warner to you ahead of a terrible punishment.
>
> [*Saba'* (34): 46]

Bukhārī records in the chapter pertaining to the commentary of *Sūrah at-Ṭūr*, on the authority of Jubayr ibn Muṭ'im (*raḍiyAllāhu 'anhu*) who said, 'I heard the Messenger of Allāh (ﷺ) reciting *at-Ṭūr* in Maghrib prayer, and when he reached this verse, *'Were they created out of nothing, or were they themselves the creators? Or did they create the heavens and the earth? No, in truth, they have no certainty. Or do they possess the treasures of your Lord or do they have control of them?'* my heart felt like it was flying!'

And other such rebukes and cataclysmic announcements from which the hypocrites were in continuous fear of, to the point that Allāh said of them,

وَإِن يَقُولُوا تَسْمَعْ لِقَوْلِهِمْ كَأَنَّهُمْ خُشُبٌ مُّسَنَّدَةٌ يَحْسَبُونَ كُلَّ
صَيْحَةٍ عَلَيْهِمْ هُمُ الْعَدُوُّ فَاحْذَرْهُمْ قَاتَلَهُمُ اللَّهُ أَنَّىٰ يُؤْفَكُونَ ﴿٤﴾

> They imagine every cry to be against them, they are the enemy, so beware of them.
>
> [*al-Munāfiqūn* (63): 4]

The verse that we are in the process of explaining, even if it is with regards to the hypocrites, consideration is given to the generality of the wording and not to the specific reason for its revelation.

'and lightning,' Allāh has set forth a similitude to lightning due to what the Qur'ān contains of the light of decisive evidences and radiant proofs. It has been made clear that the Qur'ān is a light by which Allāh uncovers the darknesses of ignorance, doubt, and *shirk*; in the same way that the natural light uncovers dark recesses. He says,

يَا أَيُّهَا النَّاسُ
قَدْ جَاءَكُم بُرْهَانٌ مِّن رَّبِّكُمْ وَأَنزَلْنَا إِلَيْكُمْ نُورًا مُّبِينًا ﴿١٧٤﴾

> O mankind! Indeed, there has come to you a clear proof from your Lord. We have sent down a clear light to you.
>
> [*an-Nisā'* (4): 174]

وَلَٰكِن جَعَلْنَٰهُ نُورًا نَّهْدِى بِهِۦ مَن نَّشَآءُ مِنْ عِبَادِنَا

Nonetheless We have made it a light whereby We guide whoever We will of Our servants.

[*ash-Shūrā* (42): 52)

وَٱتَّبَعُوا۟ ٱلنُّورَ ٱلَّذِىٓ أُنزِلَ مَعَهُۥٓ

Follow the light that has been sent down with him.

[*al-A'rāf* (7): 157]

'Allāh encompasses the disbelievers,' some of the scholars said, *'encompasses the disbelievers'* means 'destroys them,' and this opinion is testified to by the saying of Allāh,

قَالَ لَنْ أُرْسِلَهُۥ مَعَكُمْ حَتَّىٰ تُؤْتُونِ مَوْثِقًا مِّنَ ٱللَّهِ لَتَأْتُنَّنِى بِهِۦٓ إِلَّآ أَن يُحَاطَ بِكُمْ

He said, 'I will not send him with you until you swear a solemn oath to me in Allāh's Name that you will bring him back to me unless you are yourselves surrounded.'

[*Yūsuf* (12): 66]

Meaning: unless an enemy destroys you to your last man. It is said that it means 'overcome' and both opinions are close in meaning because the one who is destroyed is not destroyed until he is surrounded on all sides and their remains no way for him to escape to safety and the same applies to the one who is overcome. Also in this respect, understanding 'surrounded' to mean 'destroyed' is His sayings,

وَأُحِيطَ بِثَمَرِهِۦ

So his fruits were encircled with ruin.
[*al-Kahf* (18): 42]

هُوَ ٱلَّذِى يُسَيِّرُكُمْ فِى ٱلْبَرِّ وَٱلْبَحْرِ حَتَّىٰٓ إِذَا كُنتُمْ فِى ٱلْفُلْكِ وَجَرَيْنَ بِهِم بِرِيحٍ طَيِّبَةٍ وَفَرِحُوا۟ بِهَا جَآءَتْهَا رِيحٌ عَاصِفٌ وَجَآءَهُمُ ٱلْمَوْجُ مِن كُلِّ مَكَانٍ وَظَنُّوٓا۟ أَنَّهُمْ أُحِيطَ بِهِمْ دَعَوُا۟ ٱللَّهَ مُخْلِصِينَ لَهُ ٱلدِّينَ

...Then comes a stormy wind and the waves come to them from all sides and they think they are encircled therein; they invoke Allāh, making their faith pure for Him.
[*Yūnus* (10): 22]

'The lightning all but snatches away their sight,' meaning that the light of the Qur'ān blinds their eyes due to its extreme brilliance, in the same way that a flash of lightning almost snatches way the sight of the onlooker due to its extreme light. This is more so the case if the sight is weak because as the sight gets weaker, flashes of light affect it more severely. The poet said,

Like the day increases the sight of mortals
Due to its light and blinds the eyes of the bats

Another said,

The bats are blinded by the light of day
And the covering of the dark night agrees with them

The eyes of the disbelievers and the hypocrites are completely weak, and the severity of the dazzling lights of the Qur'ān increases them in blindness. Allāh has clarified this blindness with His sayings,

أَفَمَن يَعْلَمُ أَنَّمَا أُنزِلَ إِلَيْكَ مِن رَّبِّكَ الْحَقُّ كَمَنْ هُوَ أَعْمَىٰ

So is the one who knows that what has been sent to you from your Lord is the truth like the one who is blind?

[*ar-Ra'd* (13):19]

وَمَا يَسْتَوِي الْأَعْمَىٰ وَالْبَصِيرُ ﴿١٩﴾

The blind and the seeing are not the same.

[*Fāṭir* (35): 19]

Some of the scholar said that the verse *'The lightning all but snatches away their sight,'* means that the clear and unequivocal verses of the Qur'ān reveal the weaknesses and defects of the hypocrites.

'Whenever they have light, they walk therein but whenever darkness covers them, they halt,' Allāh sets forth a similitude for the hypocrites in this verse that when the Qur'ān agrees with their desires and expectations they act according to it, like the favours they scrounge off the believers such as their inheriting from them, their receiving a share of the war booty, and their being secure from being killed despite the disbelief that is in their hearts. Whenever it does not agree with their desires such as their being commanded to expend their selves and wealth in Jihād they falter and procrastinate. Allāh has pointed this out in His saying,

وَإِذَا دُعُوا إِلَى اللَّهِ وَرَسُولِهِ
لِيَحْكُمَ بَيْنَهُمْ إِذَا فَرِيقٌ مِّنْهُم مُّعْرِضُونَ ﴿٤٨﴾ وَإِن يَكُن لَّهُمُ الْحَقُّ
يَأْتُوا إِلَيْهِ مُذْعِنِينَ ﴿٤٩﴾

When they are summoned to Allāh and his Messenger to judge between them, a party of them immediately

> turn away. But if the right is on their side, they come to him in willing submission!
>
> [*al-Nūr* (24): 48-49]

Some of the scholars said that *'Whenever they have light, they walk therein,'* means that whenever Allāh favours them with wealth and well-being they say, 'This religion is the truth, ever since we have held onto to it we have only acquired good.' *'but whenever darkness covers them, they halt'* means that when they come across poverty or illness, or they have daughters born to them rather than sons they say, 'This has not happened to us except due to the evil of this religion,' and they apostate from it. This explanation is proven by the saying of Allāh,

وَمِنَ ٱلنَّاسِ مَن يَعْبُدُ ٱللَّهَ عَلَىٰ حَرْفٍ ۖ فَإِنْ أَصَابَهُۥ خَيْرٌ ٱطْمَأَنَّ بِهِۦ ۖ وَإِنْ أَصَابَتْهُ فِتْنَةٌ ٱنقَلَبَ عَلَىٰ وَجْهِهِۦ خَسِرَ ٱلدُّنْيَا وَٱلْـَٔاخِرَةَ ۚ ذَٰلِكَ هُوَ ٱلْخُسْرَانُ ٱلْمُبِينُ ﴿١١﴾

> Among mankind is he who worships Allāh right on the edge. If good befalls him, he is content therewith; but if trial befalls him, he reverts to his former ways. He loses both in this world and the Hereafter. That is indeed sheer loss.
>
> [*al-Ḥajj* (22): 11]

Some of the scholars said, 'Its flashing for them means their cognition of some of the truth and its darkness means the doubt that presents itself to them concerning Islām.' And Allāh knows best.[1]

[1] al-Shanqīṭī, *Aḍwa' al-Bayān fī īdāḥ al-Qur'ān bi-l-Qur'ān.*